P9-CEN-694

Praise for The Effortless Yes

Julie has gone to the heart of the matter. She clearly articulates how to convert the dreaded notion of "selling" into the joyful art of "enhancing." She shows us how to enrich the lives of those we serve by furnishing goods and services that truly enhance the life of the receiver. This book is a joy to read.

—H. Ronald Hulnick, President, University of Santa Monica

By all means, say "yes" to *The Effortless Yes* because finding yourself in chapters eight and nine is worth far more than the price of this book!

—Judith Sherven, Ph.D. and Jim Sniechowski, Ph,D.,
best-selling authors of five books, including
The Heart of Marketing: Love Your Customers and They Will Love You Back

Every woman entrepreneur needs a system for enrolling clients. The trick is, how to find a system that also aligns with a woman's values and integrity. *The Effortless Yes* accomplishes this, and more. This book will expertly guide you to getting more clients, authentically and effortlessly!

—Kendall SummerHawk, Million Dollar Marketing Coach and
Co-Founder of the International Association of Women in Business Coaching

If you are in business for yourself, you are in the business of selling. *The Effortless Yes* will show you how to serve your clients graciously and generously AND make more money than you need. Julie Steelman has revolutionized the selling conversation so that you, as your most heartfelt, authentic, and spiritual self, can lead your ideal clients and customers to THEIR Effortless Yes. I don't know about you, but that makes me, Woohoo!

—Lisa Steadman, best selling author and CEO of Woohoo, Inc.

SPRINGDALE PUBLIC LIBRARY
405 South Pleasant
Springdale, Arkansas 72764

This book is a MUST READ for every entrepreneur and salesperson. Run—don't walk—to buy it, read every word, and implement immediately. Without sales, you don't have a business, and Julie leads you in a heartfelt and compassionate way toward your gold mine. The best part is that you will discover the secret to sales that Julie taught me years ago ... and that has helped me to go from being paralyzed from fear of selling to loving and embracing the process. This book is now required reading for all of my employees!

—ANGELA JIA KIM, CEO + FOUNDER OF OM AROMA & CO. AND
CO-FOUNDER OF SAVOR THE SUCCESS

Mom business owners: Reading *The Effortless Yes* is like finding a map to a hidden treasure. Julie Steelman took me from being an under-earning wish maker to a writer with a six-figure business. If I could do it, you can, too!

—STEPHANIE VOZZA, FOUNDER OF NEVER WRITE AGAIN,
DONE-FOR-YOU COMMUNICATION SOLUTIONS FOR ENTREPRENEURS,
WWW.STEPHANIEVOZZA.COM

the *effortless*
yes

the *effortless* *yes*

**Get the Sales You Want and
Make All You'll Ever Need**

JULIE E. STEELMAN

FRANKLIN GREEN
PUBLISHING
Brentwood, Tennessee

SPRINGDALE PUBLIC LIBRARY
405 South Pleasant
oringdale, Arkansas 72764

THE EFFORTLESS YES
FRANKLIN GREEN PUBLISHING
P.O. Box 2828
Brentwood, Tennessee 37024
www.franklingreenpublishing.com

Copyright © 2011 by Julie E. Steelman

All rights reserved. No part of this book may be reproduced or transmitted in any form
or by any means, electronic or mechanical, including photocopying and recording, or by
any information storage and retrieval system, without permission in writing from the
publisher, except for brief quotations in critical reviews and articles.

Library of Congress Cataloging-in-Publication Data has been applied for.

EAN 978-1-936487-02-8

Printed in the United States of America
1 2 3 4 5 6 7 8 9 10—16 15 14 13 12 11

*To my mother and father, who worked tirelessly to teach me
to always plan ahead and do my best.*

*To my husband for being the ever-present, tireless, and
loving support I always wanted.*

*To Doctors Ron and Mary Hulnick for showing me how to
transform infinite possibility into my ultimate living ideal scene.*

And now, on to the next living vision....

contents

acknowledgments

I want to acknowledge every person who took the risk of turning their passion and purpose into a business that helps others enhance their lives. I want to thank my husband for being so supportive and patient as I spent hours inside writing this book while he wanted to play outside! I feel deep gratitude toward my spiritual mentors, Doctors Ron and Mary Hulnick, for creating the University of Santa Monica, a school the way I always wished it could be. And to my fabulous editor, Stephanie Vozza, for taking care of my words in ways no one else could. A big heartfelt thank you to Gay Hendricks for recognizing my work and helping me bring this book into being. And last but certainly not least, Angela Jia Kim for her unwavering support and willingness to hire me privately to help her grow her businesses.

introduction

Dear Conscious Entrepreneur and Business Owner:

His Holiness, the Dalai Lama, said it best, "The world will be saved by Western women." I believe that truth with every fiber of my being.

You represent the future of big business in America and around the world. If you feel inept at the cash-generating functions of your business and feel as though you have to check your spirit at the door, know that right now you hold the answer to your struggle in your hands.

Sales is the bosom of business and the life force that keeps it going. Making sales and growing your business could not be more important to your financial life.

As I sold my way out of Corporate America, I realized how much the process of selling was abused. Those negative experiences have left an imprint in the minds of women like you who, as today's business owners, struggle to create lucrative businesses without stooping to low tactics.

I wrote this book for two reasons: to give you tools to break free from anyone having financial leverage over you, and to help you break through and realize your dream of success.

The Effortless Yes is for the woman who wants to do her part to change the world for the better. This book is a culmination of my life's work and chronicles how I transformed the demands of big business into an ability to graciously serve others.

I did it by aligning my heart-set with my mind-set, using my skill-set to produce tangible results. It changed me. It changed my life. And it changed how easy making money became. In essence, I learned to sell by using heart-centered skills to help the decision-making process for my customers.

It wasn't until my later years in executive sales in Corporate America that I finally achieved my dream. All I was ever after was the ability to live financially free and never again be beholden to any person, place, or situation in order to live the way I wanted. If I could do it, so can you.

The Effortless Yes describes in detail how to strike the ideal balance between making money and helping your customers get what they want. As you reclaim your divine femininity and make the world a better place, you will play a part in altering the rules of business by bringing honor back into the buying and selling of goods and services.

The Effortless Yes will help you craft a signature sales message, claim your selling archetype, and perfect your natural selling and money-making style. Not only will you be equipped to produce extraordinary results, you will transition from feeling terrified into being gratified. You will experience a satisfying and joy-filled work life.

Make no mistake, I am selling how to sell. But I'm also selling *freedom*. I am going to show you how to own and believe wholeheartedly in the tremendous value and worth you bring to the world. When you can stand in unwavering confidence and know the truth about the gifts you want to give your customers, you will have achieved ultimate freedom. And your customers will be eager to pay you.

The objective of this book is to help you overcome your aversion to selling. To help you transcend the limitations of a fear-based mentality into the experience of profiting with a purpose. You will learn how to perform at your best, filling yourself and your business practices with heartfelt meaning and prosperity. Doing so will have a significantly positive affect on your life and all of those around you.

There are three things you need to do to get started. First, decide right now that you want to build a wildly successful business. Second, be clear that your intention is to make more money than you need in honorable ways. And, finally, choose to be willing to reveal and heal whatever stands in the way of you being able to turn any possibility into a soul-satisfying business.

I retired in Hawaii with my husband and two cats. I don't have to work to make a living, eat, or do whatever I want. I feel extremely blessed and grateful every day for this privilege.

After you finish reading *The Effortless Yes,* I trust you will feel incredibly empowered and completely unstoppable. If this book does that for you, my life will have been well lived.

Here is to you frequently hearing the Effortless Yes from your customers and claiming your ultimate bankability.

Julie Steelman

1

selling, as easy as breathing

MOST PEOPLE HAVE A DISTASTE for selling because it is grossly misunderstood. We've all been exposed to negative buying experiences and thus concluded that selling, or the act of selling, is insincere, undignified, and something to be avoided. There's just one tiny problem: businesses cannot survive unless they make sales ... and make them consistently.

Additionally, competition for the customer's dollar has increased dramatically. Entrepreneurs, the small business owners of the world, must not only sell, but sell well and find a way to do it that is normal and natural.

What's at stake? Everything. Since most entrepreneurs have a strong distaste for selling, the high rate of failure in business continues to increase, creating a vicious cycle.

Let's take a quick look at how we got here. Our country was founded on the premise of free trade with the intention of serving the common good. It's just that we ended up getting a little greedy. As a whole, businesses started off small and quickly became large, looking to sustain long-term multi-digit growth. To achieve this goal, they implemented aggressive and forceful selling tactics to reap enormous profits quickly. It worked, and other businesses adopted the same selling methods. Those early day entrepreneurial businesses became the Corporate America we know today.

Profit-making became the object of corporate worship, and serving the common good was forgotten. As a result, Corporate America quickly became a dominant force and massive consumerism was born.

Fast forward to today. Internet marketers have employed the same high-impact and aggressive sales strategies of big business, creating a society of skeptical consumers who are wary of sellers. Those cynical consumers, many of whom are women, run approximately one-third of today's entrepreneurial businesses and bring with them a strong aversion to selling. The fact is they avoid it so fervently, they risk going out of business.

Making it even more difficult to succeed is the fact most of us aren't natural-born sellers. None of us came programmed with a super-salesperson-of-the-millennium chip for effective selling prowess. Or so we think. We also don't yet recognize that the precious relationship between the buyer and seller is highly specialized. We further complicate things by duping ourselves into thinking we can continue to wing it and make tons of money by simply being charming.

Ronald E. Osborn emphasized the point when he said, "Unless you try to do something beyond what you have already mastered, you will never grow."

Selling Redefined and Refined

What if there were a new, dignified definition of selling that made it easy to sell with heart? To naturally win clients over with enthusiasm and passion? It's possible then that our businesses would not only succeed, but flourish. We would joyfully embrace selling and have viable businesses that consistently earn us a lavish income.

We entrepreneurs could overcome any aversion to selling and prosper for the long term. And isn't that why we took the risk to be an entrepreneur … to gain lifelong freedom for ourselves? After all, the heart and soul of every business is the giving and receiving of products or services in exchange for payment. Without this flow, cash flow, there is no business—only a charity or expensive hobby.

Are you ready for a new definition of selling that will change your outlook forever? Here it is:

Selling is the ability to convert customer interest into an opportunity to serve, help, or enhance another's life by offering expertise and talent—in the form of products and services—in exchange for payment.

Yes, selling is an opportunity to serve! I know that sounds radical and revolutionary; that's the point.

I developed this formula because I craved a way to bring more femininity and heart-centeredness into my workday. After earning a master's degree in spiritual psychology from the University of Santa Monica (USM) in Los Angeles, it occurred to me that most spiritual practices stay at home, never making it into the office. I decided if I was going to spend so much time at work, I wanted to create a more meaningful experience at work for me and for my customers. I started using skills such as intuitive listening to hear the deeper needs of my clients. I wanted to be of service and to help them get more of what they wanted. That took precedence over making the sale. The result? It brought everyone more happiness, including me, and gave me the meaning I was looking for in my work. Everything changed. My career skyrocketed and my income soared by over 375 percent.

The heart and soul of every business is the giving and receiving of products or services in exchange for payment.

I have used this definition of selling for years. It altered my mindset and was the key ingredient in my wild success as a corporate saleswoman. It is the number one reason I became a consistent peak performer earning top dollar. My corporate managers couldn't figure out what I was doing, nor could they replicate it. I found that the secret to selling has nothing to do with confidence or superhuman power; instead, I had uncovered my natural selling style.

And you can do what I did. You can win over customers by using your natural strengths, turning their interest into lifelong income by embracing your signature selling style. I bet you didn't know you had a signature selling style, did you? Isn't it exhilarating to think you can make money effortlessly by selling with heart, focusing on the customer, and genuinely caring about enhancing their life? Getting the Effortless Yes is as easy as breathing. We just have to take a few steps to get there.

Why Your "A-ha" Matters

You started your business because you had an "a-ha" moment that changed you. It took you on a journey to develop a product or service that would help others, too. Yet if you're like most entrepreneurs, you feel stuck because, while you loathe the idea of selling, you know you cannot sustain a viable business without making money. Adding to your discomfort is the fact that the lack of sales is really a lack of opportunity to help others. And it's the primary reason entrepreneurs start hating their businesses and give up too soon. So now what?

To be brutally honest, if you avoid selling or telling people about your products and services, you have abandoned your calling and purpose. I know it sounds harsh, but the truth is that the responsibility to fulfill your calling and mission lies within you. If you think your mission will be discovered by your customers, you will wait a long time. And you will dramatically increase the likelihood that your business will fail.

> **If you avoid selling or telling people about your products and services, you have abandoned your calling and purpose.**

Like you, I had to make a choice. I had to decide I was serious about attaining my freedom and start generating the funds I needed to do that. More importantly, I was unwilling to give up on myself and something I deeply felt called to share. The pain of failing to believe in myself and in my mission was far greater than any fear I had of selling. Think about that and make your choice right now.

The Essence of Selling With Heart

It is time to embrace the idea that tapping into your enthusiasm, passion, and heart is the most natural way to sell. It's as easy as breathing ... if you let it be. Selling with heart means recognizing the intelligence you built into your offering and confidently believing in your immense talent to help others. It also means sharing your thoughtfully created products and services with enthusiasm and caring. You step wholeheartedly into and own the inherent value incorporated into your products and services. Why? Because they deliver amazing results for your customers! Lives and businesses have been changed!

> **It is time to embrace the idea that tapping into your enthusiasm, passion and heart is the most natural way to sell.**

Right? If you don't love your products and services enough to tell people about them with enthusiasm and heart, who will?

The essence of selling with heart is understanding what selling is and what it is not. Just thinking about sales and selling can produce anxiety, but remember, it's as easy as breathing. So breathe. Let those negative thoughts slip away as you enjoy a refreshing view on how you can help others while making all the money you'll ever need.

We have redefined selling, and you are now empowered and unstoppable in achieving your dreams. From now on, every time you hear the word "sales," translate that to mean "the opportunity to help someone else get what they want." Get excited about discussing your products and services. Embrace that first moment with your prospective customer by knowing you can help them change their life. Think about how your unique story can inspire customers to want to know more about what you have to offer.

Isn't that a juicy idea? Why wouldn't you tell people how you can help them? Are you starting to get the idea that selling is a simple conversation?

Making conversation is easy … as easy as breathing. It makes sense then that selling, which is a conversation, can also be as easy as breathing. Start by educating your customers on how you can help them solve a problem, get more of what they want, and feel better about themselves. Communicate with unwavering faith the tremendous value you have for your customers. Recall your a-ha moment and demonstrate that faith by sharing stories about how you and others were transformed as a result of using your products or services. When that fervent passion comes through, you will peak the interest of your customers and inspire them to want to know more.

Speak with enthusiasm and excitement about your products and services because emotion is infectious and your customer will crave learning more. Being inspirational puts you in an influential position with your customers; you will have their undivided attention. As your customer starts to trust you, a deep and meaningful bond begins to form, giving you credibility. Therein lies the key to selling with heart; your new customer craves what you offer and wants to understand exactly how your products or services can enrich their life. They cease worrying about how much something will cost and instead focus their attention on how they can acquire what you are offering.

Doesn't that sound as easy as breathing?

Deepak Chopra reminds us how easy things are when we do what we love: "To have passion, to have a dream, to have a purpose in life. And there are three components to that purpose, one is to find out who you really are, to discover God, the second is to serve other human beings, because we are here to do that, and the third is to express your unique talents and when you are expressing your unique talents you lose track of time."

What Does a Noodle Have to Do With It?

In the early days of my selling career, I hired a sales recruiter to help me get a higher-paying job. She was from New York and had a way of saying things that didn't make much sense to me but, in hindsight, were genius. She sold advertising for *Cosmopolitan* magazine and was chic. I hung on her every word, knowing I wasn't in her league but wanting to be savvy like her.

She said to me one day in her heavy New York accent, "Julie, you never push a noodle; you pull a noodle." Huh? When I asked what she meant, she chuckled and told me to figure it out for myself.

That saying stuck with me, tumbling around in my mind until years later the light bulb went on. It explains very well how selling can be as easy as breathing. So you don't have to struggle to figure it out, I will explain.

The relationship between buyer and seller is sacred and precious. It deserves to be nurtured and held in high regard. Leading with your heart when selling is acting with honor and respect, never forcing another individual to do anything.

Respect earns higher prices while charm earns more friendships.

To counteract the negative connotations associated with selling, some entrepreneurs adopt the super sweet, overly charming method. This selling style is typically used by those who aren't skilled in sales and try to "win" business by flirting with customers. Yes, we want to build a positive relationship with our customers, but we also want to earn their respect. Acting sticky-sweet nice can be offensive to customers, because it assumes they're stupid. It can also come off as inauthentic and gross. And if we come across as overly charming, we run the risk of making a friend while losing the business.

Customers buy more frequently from people they like AND respect. A little known secret is that respect earns higher prices while charm earns more friendships. A balance between the two builds a hearty, robust business with long-term repeat customers.

To further understand what selling is, let's discuss what it is not. It's not manipulative. It isn't desperate or pushy. It's never confrontational. And it's never aggressive. Making a sale is not an act of domination, nor is it overemphasizing your point of view when your customer disagrees with you. It's never about force or lack of caring. Manipulation pushes the noodle.

Sales has been stereotyped as a man's job, and that is simply untrue. The truth is, women are wonderful sellers because their inherent nature is to take care of other people's needs. In addition, women can express things in multiple ways, complementing many listening styles. The act of selling is not about you or your goals; it is about meeting another's need by creatively using your resources. It comes from the heart.

How do you pull a noodle? To be clear, every product or service that has ever been sold provided a benefit, solved a problem, or supported an emotional need. Sales is really about respecting the other party's view and providing a solution for their needs. It's listening with your heart and understanding the customer's goals, objectives, and needs. When you know what they want, you are poised to provide them with tremendous value. The only way you can help customers is to intuitively know their real need and explain exactly how your special solution solves it.

Pulling a noodle suggests that a customer-focused approach to selling makes your offering much more attractive, thus drawing the noodle toward you. You will feel great knowing you are helping someone else get what they want. If someone helped you solve a problem or feel better, you would appreciate it. And you would probably pay for it.

Being influential and effective results in more joy for everyone involved. Selling with heart becomes an act of giving. Imagine that! Selling starts to become fun. It becomes normal and natural, giving you the ability to generously help your customers.

By being a customer-focused seller, you become an inspirational advocate for your customers and a leader. You demonstrate to others that you care. You let your customers know that working with them is much more important than the money you will make.

You must believe with all of your heart that you are the most important salesperson in your business. You have the power to make more money than you'll ever need by allowing selling to become as easy as breathing. And *that* is how you pull a noodle.

Now that you understand what selling truly is, don't you think it's time to begin?

2

demystifying how YES! happens

SELLING MAKES MOST PEOPLE ANXIOUS, nervous, or scared, because the relationship between a buyer and a seller is an intimate one. It's complicated by the fact that we often don't understand how this relationship works. It's similar to dating and wanting the relationship to result in marriage. And that feels risky.

It's tremendous fun to connect via social media and get to know each other in the public forum. It's an entirely different thing to build a deep, meaningful bond and establish trust that results in an ongoing business relationship.

Adding to the insecurity is the fact that today's buyer is more skeptical than in the past. This happened for a few reasons. First, most people received a financial wake-up call and aren't spending as frivolously as they once did. Second, they're tired of paying top dollar for hype-based promises. Finally, there is too much noise and confusion in the marketplace, including too many self-proclaimed "experts." As a result, buyers are finding decision-making to be overwhelming. And entrepreneurs, who once weren't interested in learning how to sell, are now craving the ability to do so, and to do it well.

Truth is, the only way to be affluent for life is to master the art of selling. Even if you have a sales team, you still need to know how to sell so you can effectively lead.

Before learning the seven-step Effortless YES! Selling System, you must clearly understand how the buyer's mind works. When we understand how something works—and selling is a psychological science that can be easily learned—it removes any fear you have surrounding it.

The only way to be affluent for life is to master the art of selling.

If you think about how you make a purchasing decision, the buying and selling cycle seems quite normal. Once I knew how the "sales dance" worked, it was less daunting. In fact, it became fun, building relationships in a new way and showing people how to get what they wanted.

But first you have to understand how the buyer's mind works.

The Buyer's Mind Revealed

As renown salesman Zig Zigler says, "People don't buy for logical reasons. They buy for emotional reasons." In short, buyers experience some type of pain around a specific area of their life and seek relief. What you offer is the antidote to their problem. Buyers will pay handsomely to lessen their struggle or overcome their challenge. Why? Because when they rid their source of pain, they experience pleasure.

Customers are typically focused on getting more or less of something. That excess or lack causes them pain and becomes what we call their "pain point." At some point, the pain point becomes intolerable and the customer becomes motivated to make a change. He or she is now ready to receive your help and is inspired to buy. This emotional journey is why customers respond best to solutions that promise to resolve emotional pain.

As a seller, hungry and motivated buyers make ideal customers. The more your customers are in need, the easier it is to win their business. Your product or service should clearly address your customers' needs and pains. Your customers should find it easy to understand how you can help them achieve their desired outcome.

The most common mistake entrepreneurs make in the selling process is to focus on the details versus the emotions. Service-based entrepreneurs tend to describe their process instead of the customer's emotional payoff. Product-based businesses tend to focus on ingredients, packaging, or distribution instead of how the product fulfills an emotional need.

But here's the problem: customers can't relate to processes or ingredients because they haven't experienced them yet. If you don't clearly show how you fulfill the emotional needs of your customers, they will gloss over your offer and move on to the next. It's not because your product or service isn't right for them. It's that they don't understand it yet.

Do you remember the Ultra-Brite toothpaste commercials from the 70s? The manufacturer didn't tell you how the toothpaste was made or what was in it. Instead, they created a visual emotional payoff; their toothpaste will give you sex appeal and you will get more dates!

Expressing the payoff or benefit isn't about charming your customers. It's about knowing how customers will feel after having used your product or service, and relaying that information to them before they buy.

It's not about saying what you think they want to hear; it's about completely understanding what it's like to stand in their shoes. If you don't know for sure, it's time to find out. Customers are seeking a particular feeling or experience and you have to discover what that is to communicate it clearly. (If you make this one change to your marketing and communication efforts, you will increase your business immediately.)

Remember that buyers are focused on their pain point and cannot hear you if you are talking about facts, processes, or ingredients. They can only relate to results, benefits, and outcomes!

Do you know what results or emotional payoffs your product or service provides to your customers? If not, don't worry, because we

Remember buyers are focused on their pain point and cannot hear you if you are talking about facts, processes or ingredients.

are going to address this in Chapter 4, when you claim your sweet spot. For now, start listening or noticing what emotional benefits your customers get from your products or services. Reread testimonials or thank you notes, paying attention to the words they use and the feelings they convey.

Typically, when someone is looking for a solution to their problem or wants more of something, they are laser focused on the desired outcome. They don't always care how you will help them get it as much as they care about knowing they will get it. They are singularly driven to know they will get their desired payoff before they can make a rational decision. Don't take any of that personally. Remember, they are experiencing some type of pain and want to alleviate their suffering immediately.

This brings us to the second most common selling mistake entrepreneurs make: delivering their entire sales story in one big run-on monologue. It comes out as verbal vomit and is too much information for customers to digest at one time. It overwhelms them and short-circuits their wiring. It's not the best way to start off a customer relationship, but it happens every day. The reason it happens is because sellers want to be sure they don't forget anything, so they act out of fear, assuming they won't get it right.

Remember we said that the relationship between a buyer and seller can be an intimate and delicate one. Some buyers need to take baby steps and others will move fast. The seller needs to stay in tune with the buyer's pace. Don't overwhelm them with too much information or underwhelm them with not enough facts. If you give them the whole enchilada at one time, it will be too much for them to take in and, instead of navigating through all the details, they will go away.

I like to compare this to a dining experience at a fine restaurant. The waiter delivers your drinks, then the bread, then your salad, then your entrée, and then your dessert. He doesn't bring everything all at once. If he did, you wouldn't enjoy the process and you couldn't savor each course. You would feel engulfed in too many choices, and each course would lose its appeal. It takes time for the head, heart, and body to absorb everything.

Customers are like that, too. They need time to process what you are telling them and think about how you can help them. The more they enjoy each step they take with you, the easier it will be for them to buy.

Effectively managing the sales process requires staying in the moment and listening to the buyer's needs through their decision-making journey. You want to allow enough time for your customer to mull things over but not too much time that they lose interest.

> **Effectively managing the sales process requires staying in the moment and listening to the buyer's needs through their decision-making journey.**

The Hungry Buyer Syndrome

As we continue to demystify the mind of the customer and understand how the "yes" happens, you will see that selling is one part psychology, one part finesse, and one part message appeal.

This brings us to Hungry Buyer Syndrome. Have you ever scratched your head and thought, "Hmm, I thought that customer was going to buy but she suddenly got cold feet. I must have read her signals wrong."

You've probably had an experience like this, but I'll bet those "cold feet" were really a sign of Hungry Buyer Syndrome.

Remember, most people base purchase decisions on emotions. They are starved for the emotional payoff. They want it now and rush toward the person who can fill this void. They are hungry buyers. And the more personal type of product or service you offer, the hungrier your buyers will seem.

But once the emotions feel satisfied, the brain kicks in, causing the customer to slow down and evaluate the offering. They are digesting the details. Their heart has them saying yes to your offer but their head steps in and warns them to be cautious. They get sensitive and uncomfortable, and they waiver. In reality, they are assessing and reassessing the decision to buy. What you are offering is touching something deeply personal in them, and you have to make it okay for them to choose. Sometimes their resistance to making a change or their inability to easily decide will get in the way.

As a customer makes the decision to work with you and mulls over all the variables, it's natural that they will take you on their deliberation journey. Ultimately, the deciding-to-buy roller-coaster ride is how buyers make their final choice. Unfortunately for a seller, it can be startling. The customer who came on strong at the beginning of a sale pulls away just as quickly.

Please don't misinterpret this backwards movement from the customer as a sign that your offering isn't good enough. In fact, that's far from the truth. The rush-in-and-slow-down phenomenon is a normal buyer reaction. It's a natural part of how customers cycle through their decision-making process. Embrace it. I know it feels like the exact opposite is happening and you are losing a sale. In truth, buyers ruminate on a decision when something is truly resonating with them. Buyers don't spend much time evaluating something they don't want!

Unfortunately it can wreak havoc on you as a seller because it surfaces insecurities. You can feel vulnerable and in anticipation of being rejected. You might feel your customers don't like you or that your product or service is inadequate in some way. In addition, you can start thinking your competitor is somehow better than you and has figured out something you missed. Then you start to feel sorry for yourself and want to quit.

Buyers don't spend much time evaluating something they don't want!

See how this type of thinking can quickly become a downward spiral? I know it does, because I went down that negative self-talk rabbit hole a million times. It is unproductive, and it eats away at your confidence. Learning how to achieve the Effortless Yes! is critical for two important reasons: first, you can anticipate the buyer's decision-making process and assist them through the ups and downs; and second, you overcome negative thoughts that can spawn a lack of faith in your own value.

Once I understood how the customer's mind worked, I was able to stop taking the customer's decision-making roller-coaster ride personally. I could ride the waves of the buying process, trusting it would end up well. Later, I learned to see it coming and could help buyers through it, which is what customers need you to do. The biggest reward for helping someone through the process is that it can solidify a bond with your customer.

Hungry buyer syndrome is a pivotal time in the sales process. This is when the most meaningful bond is built with your customer. Hang in there with them. Assist them to the best of your ability. If you do, you will establish a strong alliance, and your customers will feel loyal to you for graciously helping them. But if you lose confidence when this happens, so will your buyer. In fact, it's the phase of the selling cycle where business is commonly lost.

The ideal situation is that your buyer is clear in their head and their heart that doing business with you is right for them. If they act only with their heart and based solely on emotions, they are acting impulsively. Later when the brain kicks in and prompts the customer to rethink their decision, you might have to resolve buyer's remorse. Selling is much more effortless when you don't have to soothe and resell an upset customer!

Based on what we just learned about hungry buyer syndrome, you would think selling would be a no brainer. If buyers are in pain and you offer the secret elixir to resolve their suffering, shouldn't they immediately plop down their credit card?

Everyone has fears, challenges, obstacles, and issues to overcome, and these can play a role in the decision-making process. If you want your products or services to help others, you have to aid in their decision to buy. If your customers don't buy anything, you cannot help them. Selling is really a win-win when you are honest and soulful in the way you interact with your customers. Remember: selling is serving.

The Three Buying Personalities

To simplify the decision-making process, I have identified three primary types of decision makers, or buying personalities. Each has fairly predictable habits or styles and should be easy to recognize. This information made it easy for me to sell more effectively and it will do the same for you, because you will be able to best serve them if you know how to lead them. Consider this a backstage pass into the mind of the buyer!

As with anything, there are no hard and fast rules, just guidelines. You will find every buyer to be a little bit different in the way they make a decision or evaluate your offer. To best guide them, learn to detect which type you are speaking to and which phase of the decision-making process they are in.

The better you develop these techniques and use this material, the less concerned you will be with your confidence. You will be so focused on the buyer and understanding how they think that you will forget about your own worries. It's a relief to shift the focus to your customers and listen to them closely. Doing so allows you to serve them graciously and they will begin to trust you even more fully.

On the following pages, you will meet the three most common buying personalities. Once you have a better understanding of the types of decision-makers, the trick becomes identifying which one is knocking on your door. Use some of the characteristics in the descriptions to ask questions that will help you determine which type they are. You want to get as much information upfront as you can. (Avoid jumping into your sales pitch before you know anything about your customer.)

Selling well is about creating relevancy with customers and aligning your product suite with their needs. If it isn't a match for you to do business together, it is fine to say so or to refer them somewhere else. Don't accept customers with whom you don't feel a connection, especially if you are a service provider. Neither of you will enjoy the process, and things can break down. It takes moxie and character to

Buying Personality #1: The Crystal Clear Buyer

The Crystal Clear Buyer knows exactly what they want and easily makes buying decisions. They are well balanced and know how to evaluate your offer rationally and logically. They know on a gut level if buying from you is right for them. They can quickly resolve inner conflicts between their head and heart. They tend to be savvy shoppers. Some Crystal Clear Buyers want to spend time around you as they make sure you are credible.

The Crystal Clear Buyer asks all the right questions and usually has the means to buy or they wouldn't be interested. They are highly intuitive, and when they decide, their decision is typically final. Because this personality is so good at making decisions, you will rarely deal with buyer's remorse. You can easily recognize them because they will tell you exactly what they want and let you know when they are ready to buy. Another way to recognize the Crystal Clear Buyer is by noticing they have the fewest highs and lows. I find it fairly easy to recognize this type of buying personality. Their clarity is obvious and they are deliberate about getting what they want.

How to Handle the Crystal Clear Buyer

The secret to winning over a Crystal Clear Buyer is confidence. Present your offer as though you know what they are thinking. Address their questions directly and avoid straying off topic.

Explain as clearly and concisely as you can, in their language, what they get and how they get it. Make sure to share your enthusiasm about working together by telling them why you like them.

Most importantly, create a back and forth dialog. If you hog all the airtime and don't let them speak up, they will become disinterested.

Crystal Clear Buyers can be inspired to make a quick decision if they feel genuine excitement about working with you and see that you "get" their needs and fully support their cause.

Ask them if what you described fits their needs or objectives. Find out where your offer fits and where it doesn't. Make sure to ask how they *feel* about it as well as what they *think* about it.

Balance your sales pitch with emotional payoffs and poignant facts. The Crystal Clear Buyer will be insulted if you use too much charm and don't have a clearly crafted message or offer that explicitly states the key benefits.

Buying Personality #2: The Ruminating Buyer

The Ruminating Buyer thinks they know exactly what they want but finds it difficult to articulate what they need. It usually takes them longer to make a decision. Identifying this buying personality can be trickier than the others. At first they can appear to be similar to the Crystal Clear Buyer, but they become more emotional or unclear. The Ruminating Buyer is less able than the Crystal Clear Buyer to resolve inner conflicts, precluding them from making an easy decision.

Make no mistake, they are interested in your product or service, but this is their unique way of coming to a conclusion. You will discover they aren't as clear about what they need as they would like you to think.

The Ruminating Buyer has unresolved commitment phobias. They don't completely trust themselves to make a good choice. Ruminating Buyers run hot and cold. They have made costly buying mistakes in the past and find it hard to believe in any promises. They tend to hold onto their money tightly and come across as cagey when you try to clarify their needs. They aren't intentionally taking you for a roller-coaster ride, it's part of their process to say yes and no several times. The Ruminating Buyer is known for indicating they are ready to buy and promising to sign up right away. Just when you think the sale is complete, they will backtrack and want something else. They tend to display the most extreme tendencies of hungry buyer syndrome.

The Ruminating Buyer is the most volatile of all the buying personalities. They tend to have the most peaks and valleys as they cycle through their decision-making process. When you notice this behavior, there is a good chance you are dealing with a Ruminating Buyer. Don't let them frustrate or fluster you. And don't be afraid of this type as they tend to represent the largest segment of customers.

Decide at what point you think you have given them all the information you can. Politely call their bluff and ask them to make a final choice. The Ruminating Buyer requires a bit more management from you, so stick to your boundaries or you might later resent them for their level of neediness. Make sure you don't let this buying personality milk you for too much free advice.

The Ruminating Buyer can become one of your best customers. The more professionally and intelligently you handle this buyer, the more likely you will have won a customer for life. Once they trust you and see that you have their best interests at heart, it will be easier and safer for them to make a decision. They may take up more of your time, but their loyalty will pay off. Use patience and compassion as your best offense because they truly need your help and guidance.

How to Handle the Ruminating Buyer

The secret to handling the Ruminating Buyer is to understand their emotional needs and to hold their hand through the decision-making process.

They like to be led step-by-step through your materials. More than anything, they need to know for sure they can trust you implicitly.

Ask them questions that get them talking so you can understand what they need and want. Watch for contradictory statements and ask questions to clarify anything that doesn't make sense.

Empathize with their situation and validate their feelings. Be mindful of giving away too much free coaching and getting embroiled in their issues.

The way to win the business with a Ruminating Buyer is to get them to state what would make them feel comfortable enough to say yes.

Find out what is holding them back from choosing. Chances are good they hadn't thought of this, and when they give you an answer, they will see clearly how to reach a decision. This makes it easier on you both and they will see you as trustworthy. It also prevents you from giving away too much.

Use customer stories to build this buyer's confidence and belief in the benefit they will receive. Offer references if they need that extra level of comfort. By doing this you display your assuredness in your offering and demonstrate compassion for them. They will respond positively.

If you feel like you are spending too much time on this buyer, decide for yourself if you want them as a customer. If you don't, let them go. If you do, ask them to make a final decision.

Buying Personality #3: The Indecisive Buyer

The Indecisive Buyer has a passive personality and moves slowly. They are interested and yet seem disinterested. Like all buyers, if they are asking you questions and hanging around, they want something from you.

This buying personality is quiet and demure. They are savvy like the Crystal Clear Buyer but less vocal or expressive. They represent an interesting combination of smart shopper and reserved personality. At times it will feel like you have to pull information out of them. Hang in there, because eventually you will break through.

The Indecisive Buyer is comfortable avoiding decisions because they fear failure and change more than they are willing to resolve their pain. And it is hard for them to articulate this.

They need to be led to a decision and will be extremely loyal if you do it correctly. While they are intelligent, it is challenging for them to picture the end result they seek. This makes it harder for you to grasp how you can best help them. They are methodical and cautious. Since they have no sense of urgency about making a buying decision, they will sometimes fail to communicate with you.

Remember, you will have to be the leader in this relationship. Avoid underestimating their intelligence. Keep reinitiating the conversation, providing them with value and asking them to decide one way or another.

How to Handle the Indecisive Buyer

The secret to handling the Indecisive Buyer is to paint a clear picture of how their life will change for the better. Get them to see and feel the difference. Help them awaken their desire to change, and encourage them to move past their reluctance. Use influence and enthusiasm to create a sense of urgency and excitement.

pass on working with a particular client. In the end, you will be relieved you avoided a potentially negative situation and you will make room for a more lucrative customer to appear.

At the end of the day, we want to qualify our customers and understand how we best fit their individual needs. The idea is to minimize your selling efforts to the wrong customers and maximize your ability to help those who would be served best. There isn't enough time in the day to help everyone. So why not focus on assisting your ideal customer. Everyone wins!

Understanding how the buyer's mind works is one of the keys to

Gently probe and find out what they want. Dig a little deeper and uncover what is keeping them stuck or unwilling to make a decision.

Describe your offer in detail, step by step. Walk them through the progression, and explain how they will get the ultimate payoff. Make it feel easy and friendly.

Acknowledge and compliment them for being willing to investigate ways to overcome their challenge. Remember you are dealing with a buying type that tends to be fearful of change.

Talk them through their pattern of indecision and find out what decisions they regret having made in the past. Be compassionate and remind them what the lack of making a decision cost them.

Hint: What Indecisive Buyers don't realize is that not making a choice *is* a choice. By being unwilling to make a decision, they miss opportunities. Motivate them by helping them see this may be one of those times they will regret not choosing.

Invite them to talk about and visualize how their life would be different if they took the step and made the decision to buy. These types of buyers have to see the picture of how to get what they want, step-by-step.

Use the information you glean from them to construct an inspiration close and ask them to make a decision. We will discuss this in detail in a later chapter.

boosting your confidence. The lack of familiarity with the sales process creates most of the fear around selling. When you understand the normal and predictable decision-making pattern, selling becomes less awkward.

You quickly find out that selling is not about you; it's about your customer and their need to be led through an evaluation process. This, in turn, aids their ability to determine whether they want to use your product or service to solve their problem.

The truth is that a buyer's head and heart must come together in alignment before they are able to buy. The way in which that happens has some twists and turns, depending on the person. It's called the decision-making process.

The Decision-Making Process Explained

As a buyer, you evaluate many different variables as you attempt to make the best buying decision. You want to get the most for your money, but you also want to ensure that the promises being made will be kept. Right? In a competitive world with so many choices and options, you have to weigh the pros and cons of most offers. Asking questions, seeking advice, or wanting more information is natural. The same is true for your customers. They also want to get the most for their money and go through the same evaluation process you do.

In my opinion, most people dislike selling because they are uncomfortable with being the initiator or leader in the relationship. Being the leader typically creates more angst than telling people about your products or services. You know more about your products and services than anyone, and your customers look to you for assistance. If you are like most people, you can start to question your ability to lead. Then the fumbling starts and you decide selling stinks. So you avoid it. Right?

As the seller, you have to guide the relationship because customers don't know what you know. If they did, they wouldn't need you. It's your job to educate and inform them so they can make the right decision. If you don't understand a customer's thought process, the whole selling experience can feel awkward, forced, and impure. And that is what you hate and dread. Not the actual selling process and transaction. Don't worry, the Effortless Yes Selling System makes the entire sales process easy to understand and navigate.

As the seller, you have to guide the relationship because customers don't know what you know. If they did, they wouldn't need you.

Once I understood the inner workings of the buyer's mind and the steps they take to reach a conclusion, it was much easier to gracefully handle each stage of the buying process. It's simpler than you might think. Once you see yourself in it, it will make perfect sense. As you fully comprehend the buyer's decision-making process, you will switch from selling to helping.

Let's jump in and look at the mental stages a buyer goes through as they evaluate your offer. The first stage of the decision-making process is awareness. The buyer starts to notice they want more or less of something. They realize something is amiss. They become increasingly aware of a problem that is making them uneasy and/or is costing them something. That something is their "pain point" and exactly what you know how to fix. When the problem becomes big enough and unsolvable on their own, they become motivated and start seeking advice, help, and answers. The door opens, opportunity knocks, and you answer.

As customers search for solutions, they graduate from the awareness stage and enter the education stage. They start gathering and devouring information. They will read blogs and articles, browse websites, watch videos, post on social media, and search for books on the topic. The more motivated they are to resolve their challenge, the more content they consume.

As the expert with the solution, it's your job to anticipate this need and communicate in the language of your customer. Remember, at this stage of the game, they are experiencing some type of pain and will respond to messaging that assures them a solution. Take the time to master your message and name your products and services accordingly. It will reduce the effort you expend to reach new buyers. While your customers are in information-gathering mode, make as much content available as possible, so they find you first instead of your competitors.

Buyers seeking to alleviate their "pain point" want to know they aren't alone and that others have struggled with the same issue. They want to gather proof that their problem can be solved. The education phase is important, because it's when buyers are the most hungry. If they discover that you have highly desirable products that address their needs, they will want to work with you.

As buyers progress through their decision-making process, they are aware they have an issue and have gathered information about the options available. When they discover you know exactly how to help them, customers shift into the interest stage of the process.

They start to get excited and want to know firsthand what you can do for them. Either they will engage you or demonstrate an increased interest level. It's important to reach out and lead them by the hand. Make it safe, fun, and friendly to talk to you. (We will discuss this in detail in Chapter 7 on gracious engagement.)

When buyers are in the interest phase, they ask questions about you, your company, and your approach to solving their problem. This is a "buy signal," which means your potential customer is getting ready to turn their interest into action. It is the best time to build a strong relationship and begin a meaningful dialog. Ask them to explain what benefit they seek and then tell them how they will get it.

As buyers become more interested, they familiarize themselves with your personal style. They are curious about what you stand for and what qualities, commitments, and promises you bring to the table. Basically, buyers want to know why they should buy from you versus someone else. A big part of what buyers want to buy is you. They spend money with people they respect, like, and trust, which is why putting yourself and your content out there is vitally important. You minimize your efforts and maximize your rewards!

An interesting phenomenon starts happening at this point. The more comfortable the customer gets with you, the easier it is for them to move into the ready-to-buy stage. You have successfully paved the way for a decision. The goal of your messaging and offering is to create desire and a sense of urgency in your customers. You want them to want to buy immediately ... and buy from you! Each time your customer transitions to the next stage of the decision-making process, their desire to pay for relief increases.

If you have guided them through this process well, the customer now knows they can trust you to deliver the benefit they desire. The only thing left to do is to make a recommendation about how they can best utilize your products or services to get what they want.

After you've made your recommendation and you both agree that working together is the right fit, the buyer moves into the close stage. They are ready to wrap it up. Now is the time you work out the details and secure payment. Congratulations, you can start helping them overcome their struggle!

Understanding the decision-making process made me comfortable with selling. The way people reach a decision was no longer a mystery, and knowing how it worked allowed me to help along the way. I no longer felt selling was manipulation. Instead, selling was helping in the most generous way possible: to aid and support my customers' decision-making ability. When I developed the decision-making process wheel (see the model below), I could clearly understand and anticipate customers' needs at each stage.

If you stopped reading this book now, you would be well ahead of the sales game! Understanding the customer's thought process plays an enormous role in securing the Effortless Yes! By looking at the buying journey from your customer's perspective, we demystify the relationship between you and your customer. If you get stuck, keep putting yourself in their shoes and you will know what to do.

Are you ready to learn the first step of the Effortless Yes! Selling System? Great, let's get to it.

3

step one: dust off your moxie

It's Not About You

When I first started selling, I took everything customers said to me personally. I would make cold calls and hope the person on the other end of the phone wasn't interested so I could hang up and check a name off the list. That tick mark was what made me feel good. I knew I was in trouble because I was selling air conditioners and there was nothing about them that interested me. Nor did I care. Mistake number one! Can you relate?

A common reason for taking things personally when we sell is that we aren't passionate about our products or services.

Ask yourself:

- Am I deeply in love with what I'm selling?
- Does my offering reflect how much I care about helping people get what they want?
- Am I holding back enthusiasm because I think it will be perceived as too aggressive?

- Do I possess the audacity to keep selling even when my customer doesn't get it?

If you answered an unwavering "yes!" to these questions, then congratulations! You are well on your way to experiencing sales bliss. If you answered "no," it's time to change your offer into something that gets you excited ... something so juicy that you are proud to present it because it has your customers salivating.

If you are in love with your product or service and still take buyers' objections personally, it is because you care deeply about your cause. That, in turn, can make you feel less confident when you sell. Vulnerability comes from having built a business around something that is important and heartfelt to us. Of course, when our products and services reveal our personal passions, we feel more susceptible to criticism and that is uncomfortable. The truth is, when customers say "no," it has nothing to do with us and should not be taken as criticism. This mistaken mindset has us believing when our customers question our offer it equals fault-finding. In reality they are evaluating it, not us.

Years later when I started selling in person, taking things personally became a bigger problem. I couldn't hide behind the phone. I often cut meetings short and would leave crying because I thought customers were rejecting me. I didn't want my clients to see that I was too sensitive and couldn't handle their questioning my product. I mistakenly thought they were questioning me as a person. Mistake number two! In hindsight, I know they were trying to better understand the terms of the offer so they could make an educated decision. Their supposed rejection wasn't about me at all.

The truth is, when customers say "no," it has nothing to do with us.

I learned this lesson one day when everything fell apart. I had boggled an important meeting with a VIP client and got yelled at by my boss for missing my sales goals. I said to myself, "This isn't working, and I think I am the problem." It was a humbling moment. I tend to be introspective, and I was smart enough to realize that the reason I was failing was because of my mindset. It had nothing to do with anyone or anything else. I went into my famous brooding mode. I pondered the idea that something inside of me was causing this pattern and making me feel unnecessarily sensitive. My reaction to customers wanting more information about the product was too strong given the situation. I had mistakenly assumed they were rejecting me. I didn't realize they were trying to get clarity so they could make a decision.

I discovered that I didn't fully believe I had something important to say or share with my customers. I didn't own how much my product could ease their strain. I hadn't comprehended my unique ability to help my customer get more of what they wanted. And I didn't fully understand the sales cycle.

Instead, I was playing out a personal drama and looking for validation. If they bought from me quickly and easily, then I was a good person. If they didn't, then I was a bad person. I was making the entire transaction and sales process about me. A-ha! In my insecurity or need to be liked, I had set up the sales process to be about me and what I needed. Of course I was going to take the outcome personally. How could I not? Isn't it amazing how I placed myself at the center of a normal part of the selling process and predetermined the outcome?

I equated making a sale with feeling good about myself. That also meant if I didn't get the sale, I was bad and wrong. What really felt gross was the fact that I was making my interactions with customers about me. I was putting my desire to feel better about myself ahead of my customer's need to solve a problem. That realization didn't feel good at all. How could I face customers after realizing I wasn't helping them, I was looking for emotional validation?

My first instinct was to run away, change careers, and never look back. But, being a fighter, I knew that option wasn't for me. I had chosen a career in sales because I wanted the freedom to directly enhance my income. I knew I had to change the way I thought about myself and selling. If I could shift my mindset to something empowering, selling would become as easy as breathing. It would also provide me with a platform for being able to help people. I asked myself, what would be possible if I got out of my own way? What would happen if I listened to customers instead of the paranoid dialog going on inside my head?

When I took a deeper look at what I had to offer, I learned I had something important to say and I could help people in ways they couldn't help themselves. This understanding fired up my creativity. I started to see how combining my knowledge of my customers' objectives with the ability to demonstrate how the product would deliver their desired result would birth a winning formula.

Something inside me started to shift; the selling process made sense to me now. I discovered selling was a way to express my ideas and provide my customers with value. The truth about selling lit up in my mind like a neon sign. Buyers need sellers to help guide them through their decision-making process. What a paradigm shift! Selling meant I got paid to lead buyers through their decision-making process, help them understand how they benefit, and solve their problem at the same time? That sounded like a juicy win-win to me.

> I discovered selling was a way to express my ideas and provide my customers with value.

My motivation hit an all-time high. I could now see how selling was an opportunity to serve. The emotional validation I was looking for came from serving and helping others. It had nothing to do with whether or not they bought. I couldn't call clients fast enough and schedule meetings soon enough. That is when I decided to dust off my moxie, stop hoping to be validated, and get busy by taking action. I decided I had something to offer and could solve big problems. That was the value I provided. That was the juice that filled me with joy. I was motivated to help people end their struggle and gain their freedom. I no longer hoped to make a sale. I stopped waiting for sales to happen magically and I decided to do something about it. I was vibrating with a new-found excitement that would prove to be infectious. This became my first taste of becoming unstoppable and what it is like to hear the effortless yes!

The biggest lesson I learned was that what other people say, do, or think has nothing to do with me. It has everything to do with them. Funny thing, the confidence I was seeking lived inside of me, not outside of me. No one else could give it to me, and making a sale had nothing to do with me personally. What gave me confidence was having a strong purpose for selling my product. Knowing the why. I made a vow that from that day forward I would do my best to provide my customers with tremendous value and clearly show them how they could benefit from what I was selling. The biggest difference was that I decided to be of service.

> **The confidence I was seeking lived inside of me, not outside of me.**

Deciding Versus Hoping

There is a significant difference between deciding and hoping. The reason we hope to sell something instead of decide is to avoid being responsible for the outcome, dodging unwanted emotions. We would rather rely on luck than play an active role in making sales happen. Taking action to achieve what we want can cause us to feel frightened and vulnerable. Even though we say we want to run a business or earn a lavish income, we work hard to avoid doing the work that pays off ... selling.

Instead, we hope a miracle will happen and our products and services will sell themselves. We dupe ourselves into thinking we have committed to generating significant money by hoping it will come our way. Hoping, wishing, and wanting something to happen, like a dramatic increase in sales or income, is not enough to make it happen. Hope gives us a false sense of forward movement while allowing us room to bail in case we sense failure approaching. When we hope to close a deal, we are, in essence, putting fear and the lack of belief in ourselves and in our offer ahead of our desire to get what we want. Sure, windfalls occasionally happen, but they aren't bankable.

When we hope to make a sale, we give off an energy that makes customers feel hesitant to buy. Hope is the idea that something good may happen; that the desired outcome will manifest itself. The problem with hope is that it isn't always strong enough to get to yes. Hoping to make sales is like selling with our fingers crossed behind our back. If the customer says yes, we exhale and say, "Oh, thank goodness." We would rather rely on luck to close a deal than take responsibility for getting paid what we are worth.

Therein lies the problem with hope. Hope feels good. It takes us off the hot seat and lets us fantasize about our dreams coming true without having to take action. It gives us an incorrect perception of getting closer to our goal, while in reality we're just wishing something other than our biggest fear will happen. Inside that wish is a worry that we cannot make a sale or our offer isn't good enough. We don't want to face the fact that we don't fully believe in what we are selling. It doesn't make sense to say we wouldn't buy our own product or service, but a soft voice whispers exactly that. If we were confident in what we're selling, we wouldn't be wishing, hoping, and waiting for sales to happen.

Hope gives us a false sense of forward movement while allowing us room to bail in case we sense failure approaching.

Hope protects us from failure or humiliation, keeping us safe but keeping buyers away. If we were to make a whole-body commitment, a wholehearted decision to start making sales, we would have to get busy and ignore our excuses. Napoleon Hill sheds more light on the power of going beyond hope. "Desire is the starting point of all achievement, not a hope, not a wish, but a keen pulsating desire which transcends everything."

It takes moxie and willingness to make a bold decision to change our circumstances and sell in ways we never have before. There is risk involved; however, making the decision to reach a specific sales goal will put all things—seen and unseen—in motion and support the fulfillment of our goals. Without making a solid decision to dramatically increase sales, it isn't possible. How can we expect to sell that in which we don't fully believe?

The ability to decide to become responsible for generating revenue is a powerful skill. It requires us to self-source our empowerment and overcome fears and small-mindedness. When we decide to sell, we declare our offering as worthy at the price we deem fair. We step into the tremendous value we have to offer and buyers can easily understand how they will benefit from working with us. The things needed to realize our sales objectives—such as the right mindset, the right customers, and the right circumstances—start to organize themselves around us. This decision alone prepares us to take action and open up to a higher level of creativity. We uncross the "hoping" fingers from behind our back and find ways to increase our sales today. We become unstoppable.

Own It!

Selling can challenge us because we are put in the leadership position. We are the authority, and we are in charge of managing the special relationship between the buyer and seller. Most of us are uneasy with becoming the initiator. It can feel like we have an overdeveloped sense of audacity. We ask ourselves, who am I to be so bold and declare the value someone else will get? But the more prudent question, originally proposed by Marianne Williamson, is Who are we NOT to stand in our greatness and tell others about our products and services?

The truth is that the secret ingredient to selling successfully is having the audacity to declare that what you do will benefit others greatly. You must be the biggest and best advocate for your products and services. Stop taking "no" personally and start inspiring customers to make a buying decision. Fully embrace the value you offer, and let your customers see how much you believe. If you ask customers to commit to you, make a commitment to helping them. Part of that commitment is being true to your mission—expressed as products and services—and telling other

> **More sales are made with unbridled enthusiasm than with fancy strategies!**

people about it. If you don't, you fail yourself and abandon your mission. Because you aren't familiar with being in this position and you haven't dusted off your moxie, it tugs at your courage. Until today!

Here's a little secret: more sales are made with unbridled enthusiasm than with fancy strategies!

The ultimate goal of making a sale is for the buyer and seller to achieve mutual gain. You must be clear about the immense value you're offering. There is an energy exchange between the buyer and seller. You have to become aware of and responsible for the invisible undertones you give off. If you waffle or aren't sure about the value of your products and services, your buyers will feel it and become unsure. And most of them won't buy because their ability to make a decision is stifled. How you think and feel about your products and services leaves an energetic imprint on your customer.

The energy, or vibe, you give off becomes an important component of being able to make sales effortlessly. The most effective salespeople I saw in action had a clear mindset and believed wholeheartedly in what they were selling. They were unshakeable. They knew with every fiber of their being that their product or service delivered. And delivered big. They stood up into the truth of what they were selling with an unwavering belief.

You, too, can possess these qualities. Decide that your promised payoff is so important, it's worthy of enthusiasm beyond your comfort zone. Become unwilling to listen to your own excuses. In fact, when you dust off your moxie, your most popular excuses become boring. Choose to reiterate the benefit and rewards that await your buyers. Hold firmly to what you know to be true so your customers can feel how sure you are and feel justified in making the decision to buy. Are you starting to see how important our confidence is to the customer?

I have won more sales by holding my ground and remaining confident in my belief that the buyer would benefit immensely. My unfailing confidence in knowing they would get exactly what they wanted won them over. When I was unshakeable in my belief about what I was selling, my customers would decide to buy because they trusted my steadfastness. Other than my word and their ability to comprehend the facts, my buyers made their final decision based on how sure they felt. They gauged how sure they felt by checking to see if I was holding firm to my belief in my products' value.

How sure our customers feel is highly influenced by how sure we feel. Customers use it as way to affirm their decision. It doesn't matter if they say yes or no; what matters is that we take a stand for what we believe to be possible and true. That assuredness is what most buyers use to gauge the emotional validity of their choice, making a final gut check before they say yes.

In his book *Think and Grow Rich,* Napoleon Hill describes in detail how our mindset has a powerful effect on the outcome. "When Henley wrote the prophetic lines, 'I am the master of my fate, I am the captain of my soul,' he should have informed us that we are the masters of our fate, the captains of our souls, because we have the power to control our thoughts. He should have told us that our brains become magnetized with the dominating thoughts which we hold in our minds, and, by means with which no man is familiar, these 'magnets' attract to us the forces, the people, the circumstances of life which harmonize with the nature of our dominating thoughts."

Hill is telling us that we must decide how much we want to sell so it can be magnetized to us. He is giving us the mental model for attracting more clients by using our invisible abilities. The way he writes about this suggests hoping isn't going to help. He makes the clear distinction between thinking something into being versus wishing it to come true. Thinking something into being comes about as a result of deciding to make it so. The intention creates an energetic and magnetic difference in realizing our financial desires (sales) versus pining for them.

It's Time to Shine

Some of the dust particles that mar the gleam of our moxie and stop us from fulfilling our financial dreams are self-made. You know the feeling when all the surfaces in our house gleam after we have painstakingly cleaned and dusted? The same is true when we embrace our mission and boldly serve others with our products and services.

Dusting off one's moxie is an ongoing process. In this moment, set aside the fear and doubt and make a firm decision to increase

SPRINGDALE PUBLIC LIBRARY
405 South Pleasant
Springdale, Arkansas 72764

your sales as much as you want. Move out of hope and into decision. Stop waiting and take action toward your desires by honoring yourself and your customers. Begin to sparkle and fully believe that the value you offer is something your customers crave. Dust off your moxie and step into the empowered audacity waiting for you.

We all can sell brilliantly. We simply have to choose it. Pick one benefit your customer will get when they buy from you, and start talking about it. Keep adding to the list as you become more comfortable.

If you learn one thing about dusting off your moxie, let it be this: Selling isn't about doing what is easy and quick; it's about providing value in exchange for deserved payment. Do yourself a big favor and stop hoping. Instead, decide to make more money than you'll ever need by putting on your big girl panties and opting to dust off your moxie.

Six Steps to Dusting Off Your Moxie

1. In your journal, write two sentences about why you care that your customers resolve their challenge, alleviate their pain or struggle, or get more of what they want.
2. Based on the information from the first step, write a clear statement that captures the heart of why you are selling your products or services.
3. Post this statement where you will see it often. Recite it frequently until it becomes your mantra. The next time (and every time after that) you start to take "no" or "not right now" or "I don't have the money" personally, recite your mantra and remind yourself why you are doing this.
4. Answer these questions honestly: Have I been hoping to make sales? Have I been waiting for something to happen? Have I believed my own excuses, or societal stories, about why it's hard to make a sale?
5. Determine which moment in dealing with a customer gives you the most juice. List five ways you can start creating more of those juicy moments.

6. If you are willing, decide right now that you are going to take responsibility for making sales. Decide, clearly and firmly, that you are releasing the wanting, wishing, or hoping to make sales. Write this commitment statement in your journal:

   As of this moment, I, (fill in your name) am no longer willing to use any excuses to stifle my sales momentum. Instead, I declare that I have completely and clearly decided to increase my sales dramatically and take responsibility for doing so. My intention is to listen to myself, serve my customers generously, and invite them to do business with me no matter what. I claim my deserved right to experience the effortless yes.

4

step two: claim your sweet spot

THE PURPOSE OF CHAPTER 3 was to help you gain the courage needed to clarify the heart and soul of your bigger message and embrace the value you offer your customers. Additionally, it was designed to set you up to own the uniqueness of your story, mission, and brand, because that is what you are truly selling (and your customers are buying) at the deepest level.

For me, the ability to claim your sweet spot is one of the most gratifying parts of being able to sell. Our story is what fills our message with heart. Something magical and magnetic happens when we identify with and own our story. A newfound confidence that translates into radiance becomes obvious, mostly to customers, but also to ourselves. We begin to attract the ideal customer: one who can afford our products and services and is willing to invest in getting the improvements they seek.

Remember when we talked about how the vibe we give off plays an important role in helping customers decide to say yes? Claiming our sweet spot, the unique and lavish benefit we offer our customers, becomes the juice we need to stretch and grow. It also significantly boosts our selling prowess. I always say, "In order for your business to grow, you must grow."

Once you know exactly how you serve and deliver the promised benefit, you can easily identify your distinctiveness. Your notable competitive advantage emerges. Name that uniqueness in a way that has customers salivating and craving your offer because it hits home.

In order for your business to grow, you must grow.

The name you give your products or services is the first thing new customers notice. The name should include the payoff or expected result they seek.

Your job is to tell them how you deliver that promise. When you sell from this perspective and absolutely love what you are offering, selling becomes much more normal and natural. I had a client say to me one day, "Julie, I look forward to the day when selling feels as easy as breathing." That is exactly where we are headed. Guess what? When you claim and name your sweet spot, selling will feel effortless.

What Is a Sweet Spot?

Your sweet spot is the thing you do so well no one else can do it in the same way. It is where your life experience, talent, knowledge, and expertise intersect to form products and services based on your distinct ability to resolve your customers' challenges. It is infused with your personal story.

Your sweet spot is the place where your persona, creative solutions, and customer payoff converge to create a transformative elixir. That elixir aids your customers by eliminating their challenges, removing struggles, and/or improving their ability to exceed their objective. It also provides your customers with a potent positive emotional experience for which they sought you out.

Your sweet spot is the thing you become known for. It is the thing you love most about yourself and your business. It becomes the signature and the hallmark of what you do. It builds your business exponentially because customers seek you out for it. The sweet spot is the essence of your brand. The way to claim it is to name your expertise or specialty, describe for whom it's meant and clearly state how it delivers on its promise (or what I call your unique payoff proposition).

Your sweet spot is the thing you become known for. It is the thing you love most about yourself and your business.

Knowing it and naming it makes it all that more real for you and your customers. It is your specialty and highlights your brilliance. A clearly defined sweet spot creates a niche within a niche, making you all that more relatable. Customers will instinctively know they want to work with you or buy from you because of your ability to help them get what they want. It is this memorable uniqueness that makes you stand apart from competitors or those who claim they do what you do.

Your sweet spot usually represents the thing you care most about helping people resolve. When you are in your zone or on your game, amazing things happen and magic gets created with your customers. Sometimes nailing down your sweet spot takes time and thought. For others, it may be more obvious.

Your sweet spot, or what Gay Hendricks calls in his book *The Big Leap* our "zone of genius," is a microscopic, intrinsic thing that produces powerful results while enhancing the lives of others. Gay explains the zone of genius like this: "Your zone of genius is the set of activities you are uniquely qualified to do. They draw upon your special gifts and strengths. Your zone of genius beckons you with increasingly strong calls as you go through life."

When you look closely and discover how you facilitate a transformational moment for your customers, how you precisely help them breakthrough or up-level, you will find your sweet spot. You will also find an infinite supply of compassion and understanding for the problem you are attempting to help resolve, because you have been there yourself. It is no accident that your sweet spot, or what you do best, is reflective of your own story.

How can you sell or offer help unless you have lived it and resolved it for yourself first? Your sweet spot is a precious and sacred gift you share with your customers because it is a core part of you. It comes from the soul. It's something you have or do that your customers would like to replicate. It's the core essence of what you are selling. Doesn't that feel good?

Who, Me? Work at Microsoft?

Back in early 1999, I was selling online advertising for a popular sports website, CBS Sportsline.com. It was a fun job because we took customers to the Super Bowl and met all kinds of celebrity athletes. We were part of an exciting e-commerce launch for an online sports equipment store called MVP.com. Michael Jordan, Wayne Gretzky, and John Elway were the front men. At the launch party, I shook hands with Muhammad Ali and danced with Evander Holyfield. Being from Chicago and an avid Bulls fan, I wanted to meet Michael Jordan, but I couldn't get near him.

These were thrilling times in my career, and yet I felt something was missing. My team and I were having tremendous sales success (not to mention a lot of fun doing things others only dream of), yet the working environment left something to be desired. It wasn't female friendly.

One day a recruiter I knew called and said she needed to speak with me urgently. She had been trying for months to get me to agree to fly to Seattle and interview with Microsoft for a sales management position at MSN in Los Angeles. I kept putting her off. I couldn't picture myself working at Microsoft; I was too much of a nonconformist to fit in. I didn't realize it at the time, but I was intimidated and used the "too many rules" argument to avoid accepting the interview. Somewhere inside a nagging voice was replaying the old story, "you aren't good enough either."

I was known for making trouble, being more of a maverick then a corporate suit. I didn't think I would fit in at MSN. The recruiter kept pushing me, telling me Microsoft was a great place to work and that I would like the eco-system. She wouldn't let it go and said she knew instinctively this was my next job. She finally got through to me and, since I had nothing to lose, I agreed to go on the interview.

A few weeks later, I landed in Seattle and was scheduled to spend a full day interviewing with eight different people. They call it "running the gauntlet." The truth? I had an incredibly fun time and thoroughly enjoyed the day. I met the most vibrant and intelligent people I had come across in quite some time. I found myself feeling smitten about the possibility of running the LA sales office for MSN. Before leaving Seattle, I had decided I wanted the job.

My special blend of understanding buyer psychology and bringing out the best in others' sales ability was exactly what they were looking for. I didn't know until after "running the gauntlet," but I was looking for them, too. I had been seeking more than a job; I was looking for a company where I could thrive and grow. Where I could claim my sweet spot as a leader and be supported in developing it further.

I loved what I was hearing. These guys were no-nonsense, focused on getting business done and helping everyone succeed. Being the legal lightning rod of the country, Microsoft had worked hard to create a safe and comfortable working environment where unsavory behavior wasn't tolerated and gender issues were minimal. The more I interviewed with the sales management team of MSN, the more I was hearing myself own my uniqueness and specialty.

The story ended well and after much negotiation, I accepted the job. It took a few weeks for it to sink in that I had just been hired by Microsoft.

I discovered a lot about myself that day. I had a unique gift: the ability to facilitate "a-ha" moments for customers and my sales staff and translate them into money. When you spend an entire day talking about yourself and what you do well, you claim your sweet spot.

As I look back over my corporate career, I see that this was a defining moment. As soon as I was willing to accept my true value and worth, selling became much easier and I started getting paid in alignment with the value I provided. I possessed the confidence I had always been chasing. Claiming my sweet spot was a breakthrough for me, and I started making more than I would ever need.

If I can do it, you can, too.

Your Unique Payoff Proposition

You've seen how powerful claiming your sweet spot can be. It's the difference between faking it or making it. The challenge lies in translating that special thing you do into words that strike a cord with your customers. What you offer has to resonate with them powerfully. Your message has to speak to their head and their heart or they will gloss right over what you have to say.

One of the most important aspects of selling effortlessly and experiencing a soul-satisfying business is to succinctly explain the payoff your customers get. That is called your unique payoff proposition, and it has two distinct parts. The first is the tangible result they get from working with you, which appeals to their head. The second is the emotional boost they receive from using your products and services, which is pleasing to their heart. When you can say with sincerity how your products and services deliver both components, you will dramatically reduce customer resistance.

The unique payoff proposition works like a charm because it resonates with your customers on a soulful level while helping the brain understand what it gets.

In the traditional sales world, this is called your "unique selling proposition." I'm going to call it your unique payoff proposition, because I want you to focus your attention on what the buyer gets. It also takes the pressure off you having to persuade someone to see things your way. When communicated in this way, the unique payoff proposition instantly lets the customer know what they get from you.

To make a distinction, your sweet spot is that thing you do so well you would do it for free. It is yours. Your unique payoff proposition is how your specialty translates into benefits for your customers; what customers get as a result of your operating from your sweet spot. The two combined are a surefire way to win repeat business.

When you claim your sweet spot, you be- **It's more important** come a living example of what you are selling. **than ever to clarify** You give off an energetic vibe because spiritu- **your unique payoff** ally, mentally, emotionally, and physically, you **proposition.** have mastered something your customers want. You have put the unique payoff proposition into action, and it has come alive in your customers' minds. When your customer understands what both their head and heart will get, you have the ultimate payoff proposition!

Remember, customers buy based on emotional needs and actually hand over the money when their head says yes. Knowing this, it is important to distill your message down far enough so you speak to both parts. A big part of how your offering is evaluated is based on being true to your message and living the desired outcome. Customers will connect to your story, which creates a trusting bond and shows them that what they want is achievable. It endears you to them.

Make no mistake, every one of us has a special and unique offer. Some customers will be attracted to working with us while others are more comfortable working with someone else. Even so, there is enough to go around. Yes, some people are better sellers than others. However, today's skeptical are tuning into you and the authenticity of your message. It's more important than ever to clarify your unique payoff proposition.

Play the "So What" Game

One of the most profound things I learned in my many years of corporate sales was to play the "so what" game. The big companies I worked for spent hundreds of thousands of dollars on sales training and most of it didn't stick. The thing that did stick, however, was the way to make our message compelling by playing the "so what" game with our sales story.

We used to spend hours sitting around the conference table doing this with our presentations so they were strong, clear, and enticing. It only mattered that the message had a powerful impact on the customer, not that it sounded great.

The trick is to be able to articulate your key points in your customer's language, not yours. Which is why the "so what" game works so well. It forces you to stand in your customers' shoes and determine why they would care about what you are telling them. Customers are trying to discern what your offer will give them, not why you designed it the way you did.

For example, so what if your awesome body products have lavender in them. So do many others. But if you told me the lavender you use will make my skin softer and melt away stress, you will create a distinction for your brand that makes it easier for me to decide to buy it. You will also earn my loyalty because you made my decision-making process easier.

Paint the picture for your customer that shows them how your product or service is different. They won't take the time to figure that out for themselves, nor should they have to. If you make them work to figure out how they win, they will move on to the next thing. Customers want to be able to tell quickly and easily what they get or they are gone.

The "so what" game will help you nail your unique payoff proposition. Start by listing the emotional quality and the tangible results you promise. Now ask yourself, "so what?" Each time you answer "so what," you will arrive at a more refined meaning of what you're promising. Eventually, you will arrive at the most significant benefit and your unique payoff proposition will be revealed.

The other benefit of doing the "so what" game is you will have a number of ways of saying the same thing. As you speak with more of your customers, you will find which phrases hit home. The "so what" game is one more way of eliminating any faltering on your part from the selling process. It allows you to talk about your products and services in fresh, new ways that you feel good about and customers understand.

Step Two: Claim Your Sweet Spot

An Example of the "So What" Game in Action

Coaches might say, "When you work with me you will get tons of clarity."

While that sounds great and like something your customer might be looking for, it warms their heart but doesn't speak to their logical side because it isn't tangible enough. As we discussed, a buyer cannot make a decision to spend money with you based on the idea they will get more clarity.

Now ask yourself, "So what if they get more clarity? What does that mean for them and their business?" You should be able to come up with a more well-rounded answer. You might find that getting clarity has many positive implications for their business. It's possible they might find a new income stream, they might be more excited, they might be able to stop doing work they don't like, they might be able to save their customers time and money by developing a more efficient process or they might be able to stop feeling lost or over-whelmed. There are endless possibilities, but it's up to you to hone your message. It is vitally important that you know exactly what you mean when you describe both the tangible and intangible outcomes of your offering.

Let's take this a step further so you can see how powerful this game is.

Initial statement: When you work with me you get tons of clarity.

So what if I get more clarity, what does that mean for me? You will save time because you know what you want to do.

So what if I save time, what else does that do for me? In addition, to saving time, you will find an increased sense of satisfaction because you are efficient and able to zero in on exactly what you want to do.

So what if I have an increased sense of satisfaction and can focus on what I want to do? You will be able to intelligently, gracefully, and instantly develop a product suite you are ecstatic to talk about. Not only will you find more joy and satisfaction in your work, you will be able to generate business more easily.

Revised statement: When you work with me, you will get tons of clarity. What that means to you is you will possess the ability to tap right into the heart of what you want to do and the perfect product suite that attracts your ideal customer will unfold. The biggest benefit of having more clarity is you save time while boosting your spirit and increasing how much joy you feel. That naturally translates into more business for you.

Bingo! Pay dirt! Now how does that sound? Would you want to buy from this coach if she explained why you should care about clarity like that? The revised statement is exciting. See how much easier, as the seller, it would be to talk about?

In this example, we went from trying to win business based on offering a customer clarity to telling the customer that their heart will like this because it gets to feel more joy, while letting their brain understand how clarity will save them time, allow them to develop an attractive product suite and make them more money. All of a sudden your offer sounds super juicy and compelling. It makes the buyer want to plop down their credit card because they are tired of feeling foggy and fumbling for answers. They want to make their ache disappear and you just told them how that can happen! The unique payoff proposition did its job.

• • •

The "so what" game is a powerful tool and it helps you get to the most profound part of your sales story, your ultimate unique payoff proposition! Repeat the process a few times until you hit the emotional payoff and external reward, then you know you have reached the core of your offering. You will become intimately familiar with your distinctive advantages, making you a stronger and more confident seller. When you can take a step back and see just how much people get from doing business with you, you will feel delighted to share your sales story.

Playing the "so what" game gives you a distinctive advantage in how you position yourself and what you are selling. It forces you to focus on what the buyer gets and find a way to phrase it in their language. Customers will ask questions in different ways. The "so what" game will reveal all of the features, benefits, and payoffs of your own products and services, allowing you to handle objections and lead your customer through their decision-making process.

As a seller, everything you do or say has to be about the buyer. Until they ask about you, talk about them. Discuss what *they* will get for their money, how *they* will feel and what material results *they* could get. Specify what will be different for them. Telling your sales story in this way makes it easier to sell. In fact the "so what" game is my secret weapon to being falter-free. It is much harder to be stumped by customer questions if you use this technique.

Declare Your Right to Be Audacious

Naming and claiming your sweet spot is one of the most important steps you can take to win business. Selling becomes effortless because you are in love with what you are doing, know exactly how to describe it and can offer the best option for your customers. Can you see how your sweet spot combined with your unique payoff proposition becomes the best "salesperson" on your team? It is a powerful combination because it gives your customers an inner sense that you can help them in a way no one else can.

Declaring your sweet spot isn't complete until you own it, are proud to talk about it, and can articulate how customers will get what they want. The natural next step to take is to declare your right to be audacious. You, yes you, have something profound and wonderful to share with the world. The audacious Steve Jobs said, "I want to put a ding in the universe." And look what he has done! If you don't tell anybody about how you can help them get more of what they want, how will you ever stay in business, much less fill the need that is driving you?

When you don't tell your story or show others how they can enhance their lives by using your products or services, you withhold the opportunity for your customers to have a breakthrough. It

Claim your sweet spot and name your unique payoff proposition so you can fulfill your most important mission ... to be of service in your special way.

doesn't feel good to hear that, but it's the truth. You were gifted with an ability to make life easier for others through your products and services. But many of us would rather hide than spread the word because it might come off as arrogant, right?

Well, guess what? Your customers are clamoring for your help. They want you to lead them and be the authority you are. And you have the right to boldly proclaim your greatness by opening your mouth and confidently sharing your talents. You cannot serve, help, assist, coach, guide, enhance, or improve any of your customers lives if you don't claim your sweet spot. Immerse yourself in the fact you are a remarkable force in the world and your business is how you spread that around. Claim your sweet spot and name your unique payoff proposition so you can fulfill your most important mission ... to be of service in your special way.

Eight Steps to Claiming Your Sweet Spot

1. On a fresh sheet of paper, write down your expertise, your specialty, what you excel at, and what you would love to be known for.

   Example: My expertise is the ability to close almost any deal. My specialty is teaching women how to sell graciously and gain their freedom. I am known for transforming "a-ha's" into long-term bankability.

2. Now play around with word choice and put together phrases that name your uniqueness. Use a thesaurus and interchange words until it feels like the perfect fit. Keep at it until it feels right and you get excited. (Note: do a quick Google search to see if anyone has already branded that name.)

   Example: The Selling Expert, The Sales Sage, The Selling Diva, Sales Superstar, Selling Mentor

3. Next write down at least ten characteristics of your ideal customer. Make another list of what they want from your products or services. See if you can identify a commonality and give it a name.

   Example: My ideal customer is an entrepreneur, female, well-educated, upwardly mobile, ambitious, spiritual, and ready to make it big. She comes to me because she hates to sell and knows she needs to or she will go out of business. She avoids the selling process and thinks selling in any form diminishes her spirit.

4. Take the results from step two and combine them with the client descriptions. Play with more phrases until you get close. Name the group your customer represents or include a word or two that demonstrates how you help your customer improve. Doing this exercise helps you claim your sweet spot and helps customers understand quickly what you do.

   Example: My customers are entrepreneurs, and I want most to mentor them into realizing purposeful prosperity. Some options are: The Female Business Owner's Selling Sage, Entrepreneur's Selling Diva, Bankability Guru, Your Sales Super Star. I picked: The Entrepreneur's Selling Mentor.

5. Set that aside and make a new list of what customers can expect or what results are normally produced when customers buy from you. Be as specific as you can. List out the deliverables you promise and think about how those things make your customers feel. List those feelings too.

6. Taking that list of tangible results and emotional feelings, play the "so what" game with the top two on each list. Go at least three rounds for each topic and write down what you come up with. When you feel like you have hit pay dirt, make a note of it and start using those statements in your posts, web copy, and personal conversations.

7. Write a revised payoff proposition statement. Write at least two

different statements, including the inner and outer components. Post these someplace where you will see them often and start using them.

8. Take the answers to your "so what" questions and form a story. Take a look at this before and after:

   Before: *"I specialize in helping customers like you get clear about what you want to offer. My process is designed to take you to the point of knowing exactly what you do best and then putting into form."*

   After: *"One of the things I do best is help my clients get clear about what they are offering. That clarity translates into saving time, money, and energy when developing their product suite. And, the best part is, when you have that kind of clarity, you will fall in love with your business again because you recapture the fulfillment and joy you once had."*

   Which sales message would you respond to?

Complete these exercises before you read the next chapter. We are going to use what you came up with to make your pitch irresistible!

5

step three: craft your irresistible pitch

NOW THAT YOU HAVE CLAIMED your sweet spot, you are probably already seeing a lucrative niche that has your name written all over it. Own it! And if you think back to the decision-making process model in Chapter 2, you know that you will have to make your pitch to your customers. But contrary to what most people think, crafting your pitch in advance is a must. Not only does it give you an advantage, you will feel more comfortable delivering it. "Winging it" is out of the question if you want to make sales effortlessly.

You've probably already put some thought into constructing your pitch. You might love what you have or you might not. The most misunderstood part of the pitch is its purpose. Most people think an elevator pitch, or what I call the quick pitch, has to close the deal. That is not its intention. Your quick pitch is meant to peak a potential customer's interest.

Quick pitches, which are used in casual settings like networking events or phone conversations, should interest and intrigue. A great quick pitch is enticing enough that the listener immediately wants to know how to get some of what you are selling.

The primary function of the quick pitch is to get past the initial permission barrier and gain the listener's attention. Once you have their buy-in to continue, you will have an eager-to-pay-you customer, the best customer mindset you could hope for. It makes starting an in-depth sales conversation easier.

Getting Past the Permission Barrier

The permission barrier is that radar or defense mechanism most people have to protect themselves from awkward sales situations. When a quick pitch sounds inauthentic or the listener doesn't believe you or has no interest in what you do, you might as well be talking to a fence post because you've run smack into the permission barrier. When you get the listener to lower their permission barrier and give you a signal to continue, you've lowered their defense mechanism. They open up, listen closely and show interest. They are receptive to your message, and it's as if they invited you to tell them why they should buy your product or service.

There is a graceful, respectful, and tactful way to get past the permission barrier. When you introduce yourself to someone or are in a situation where you might talk about what you do, lead with a compelling sentence. Next, qualify their interest level by asking them a question. By bringing them into the conversation, you can quickly learn something about why they might be interested and gain permission to tell your story. This instantly unlocks the permission barrier. This is the ideal situation in which to make your quick pitch, because now you are speaking with someone who cares about what you are saying.

Now that you know how to overcome the permission barrier, we are going to talk about creating an irresistible pitch. Not only will it grab the listener's attention, it can turn them into an interested customer. Knowing how to craft a compelling pitch allows you to have a flexible message and be quick on your feet. And part of being super-successful at selling is the ability to respond intelligently on the spot.

In a more formal setting, where you're presenting to prospective buyers or investors, your pitch should also be provocative and compelling. It would show the customer why buying from you will positively affect their circumstances. In a formal situation, you would have done research and constructed a customized pitch for your meeting. While you can use the steps in this system, the difference is that you would know something about the people you'll be meeting with and what their needs are. Use that information to create an irresistible formal pitch. Keep checking in and getting permission to keep going. Your customers will respect you for checking that they're still interested. And you will want to know if you lost them before you get to the end of your presentation.

For our purposes, we are going to talk about how to construct your quick pitch. The reason you want to develop your pitch before speaking to a customer is so you can direct the conversation and make the best use of the time you have together. Also, you want to feel comfortable and confident in what you are saying, and knowing your pitch in advance allows you to build a consistent and strong message while describing what you do. As you tune in to the verbal and non-verbal responses of your listener, use that information to keep the conversation going. Before you know it, they will ask you to tell them more.

Components of an Irresistible Pitch

Let's get started by understanding what makes up an irresistible pitch. Ray Kroc says, "If you work just for money, you'll never make it. But if you love what you are doing, and always put the customer first, success will be yours." I would add that being enthusiastic about your products and services adds a unique element of enchantment to your quick pitch, making it irresistible!

Plenty of people offer the same service or product that you do. How you convey your message is what will distinguish you and make you memorable. As Simon Cowell of American Idol fame says, "You have to make it your own and tell us who you are."

The same thing applies to your pitch. Remember: More sales

have been won through pure enthusiasm than fancy pitches. The next few paragraphs will take you step-by-step through the process of crafting your irresistible pitch. The steps are more about getting you excited than giving you a formula for a fancy pitch. How well you influence your listeners has everything to do with how enthusiastic you are when you deliver your pitch.

As potential customers find you, they can get information about you all over the Internet. Those words have to replace your personality on a web page. They might be effective but they will never be as powerful as speaking to your customer in person. If you have the luxury of talking to your potential customers live, make that meeting positively noteworthy. If you do, you will have the opportunity to turn that conversation into a lasting connection, one that outlives words.

You won't get many second chances to make a first impression, so make it a great one. Get people interested in what you have to offer by personalizing your pitch just enough to develop a bond. However, avoid talking about yourself or your business too much, or it can come across as self-absorbed.

There are five components to an irresistible pitch. They have been real-world tested and work well. As you start to write, notice what gets you excited to share. Set an intention to write a quick pitch that feels good to say and catches your listener's attention. Say it out loud to yourself and see if you would be interested. If so, congratulations! You have passed the self-pitch test. If not, don't worry. Keep working on it.

The Five Components of an Irresistible Pitch

- A clear and concise explanation of what you do best
- A translation of how what you do benefits your customers
- An honest statement about why you do what you do or why you care about helping others
- A question that pulls the listener into the conversation
- Words and language that appeal to your ideal customer, engaging their heart and ensuring their mind

Did you notice something? These components combine your sweet spot and unique payoff proposition into a captivating story that grabs your customer's attention! All we did was put them together and add in a biographical element to personalize the pitch. It is important to remember to tell people why you do what you do. It prompts questions and comments from the listener, and humanizes your pitch, removing any "salesy-ness" from it. It keeps your pitch from sounding pitchy (no pun intended) and makes new acquaintances more inclined to lower their permission barrier.

When you ask the listener a question and pull them into the conversation, they will trust you more. All of a sudden you just shared your pitch, told them something personal about you and turned it into an opportunity to take the conversation a step further. See how effortless that feels?

Making It Irresistible

There are three ways to add flair to your pitch, making your listeners excited and eagerly wanting more. First, let your customers know you "get" them and empathize with their situation. The easiest way to do this is speak in their language and sensitively talk about their pain points. Second, let customers know how their lives will improve by buying your product or service. Spice up your word choice to make them hungry to find out more. Your unique payoff proposition statement accomplishes this nicely. Lastly, let your customers know why you care. This is what sets you apart and helps the customer's decision-making process.

The more you can personalize, or humanize, your pitch, the more irresistible it becomes. When these three things work harmoniously together, your pitch becomes compelling and leaves a lasting first impression. Often, if your pitch is strong and you deliver it with confidence, the listener will decide on the spot they have to work with you. That is the ideal situation, but it doesn't happen every time.

A quick pitch that sounds like a memorized flash card will work against you and won't feel right for either of you. I am sure you can think of moments when someone delivered a pitch that had a negative effect. Today's buyers are savvy and have a lot of options to consider. They are tired of getting less than they expected and have become skeptical and discerning. When they first meet you, they will try to determine—consciously or unconsciously—if you are trustworthy. They want to know you are human, the real deal. They will judge whether you have the credentials to honestly help them or if you're just selling something to make a buck. Their radar is strong; don't trip over an opportunity to help someone by coming across as disingenuous.

The fastest way to enchant your listener is to tell enough of your story so you earn their trust to take the next step. Give them something to relate to—a little insight into how you overcame your challenges—and they will start sharing their own story. That is how the sales conversation starts.

Your story, or the "a-ha" moment that had you drop everything and decide to create your product or service, is what gives you credibility. It instills confidence in the listener, which leads them to believe you deserve a few more minutes of their time. Your story becomes a natural conversation starter. It gives the listener something they can relate to. They love that you brought the subject up, and if they have something to say about it, they will tell you. Before you know it, the two of you are in a deep and meaningful conversation, without you feeling awkward or nervous.

As you continue your conversation, you reveal more to each other. Once you have insight into your listener's dilemma, it's easy to determine if they're a potential customer. And then it becomes easier to find ways to apply your product or service to their needs. Exactly as they need it.

The fastest way to enchant your listener is to tell enough of your story so you earn their trust to take the next step.

Yes, it's really that simple. I bet you do this every day, giving advice without even realizing it. Selling is the same thing! Pitching in this fashion is how you bond with your customers. The truth is, what makes your pitch irresistible is you. Your special offer helps sweeten the outcome, but if the customer doesn't get a sense of you, the payoff, or why you are doing this, there won't be an emotional connection. And no emotional connection usually means there is no sale, regardless of how sweet the deal.

Selling is an art, and these formulas will become your tools. Incorporate new things your customers tell you along the way and tweak your pitch as needed. Keep listening to your customers. Make sure to note when you hear things repeatedly. That means it is a common struggle, so use it. It makes you relatable when you pitch and removes the "she's selling me" thought from the listeners mind. Before long you won't even remember those uncomfortable moments you used to have.

Write out your pitch and keep working with the wording until you want to pump your fists and exclaim, "Yes!" Once you think you have it, stand in front of the mirror and repeat it. Did you like it? Did it make you feel great? Would you want to hear more if you were the customer? You should feel excited to share it. If not, keep working on it. Trust the process. It will come to you.

• • •

Let's talk more in-depth about the fourth component of an irresistible pitch, the question that pulls the listener into the conversation. It's what makes the difference between gaining new customers or being perceived as the chick canvassing for business. Adding a question lets you gauge how your quick pitch is being received. People love to talk about themselves, and they will remember most what they said, not what you said. When they know more about you and can relate to you, they will open up more quickly. If you get them talking, not only will you glean insightful information, they will most likely remember their conversation with you.

I know that sounds a little contradictory to what I just said about telling your story, so let me expound. The intention of your quick pitch is to get the listener to open up and be willing to hear more about your

People love to talk about themselves, and they will remember most what they said, not what you said.

products and services. When you do that, they drop their guard. People record in their mind's archive what they said. They remember the energetic imprint or feeling tone they left the conversation with. They will remember the impression you left more than they will remember details of what you said. If they can relate to you or parts of your pitch, they will remember you as someone who can help them get what they want. That is what creates an association in the customer's mind between you and the solution to their problem. You will want to be a part of what they remember because the first hurdle to making a sale is complete. Having moved past the permission barrier and into the zone of interest, you have created a viable opportunity to win the business. That is the ultimate goal of the quick pitch. Does this seem much easier now?

Constructing the Quick Pitch Question

The way to construct the quick pitch question is to think of the most common scenarios in which a customer would reach out to you. Think back to conversations you've had with your customers. What pained them the most? What resonated with them the most? What common struggles did they have? How does that struggle make them feel? Start turning the things your customers say into questions that create a dialog with new customers.

Create some pre-planned questions and memorize them so you are ready when the right opportunity arises. Here are some ideas to get you started:

1. Ask if _____ has ever happened to them.
2. Ask if they use what you are selling, or if they are happy with it.
3. Ask if they've ever thought of using or buying what you sell.
4. Ask them if you could show them how to have more _____ in their life, would they be interested in hearing more.

As you can see the possibilities are endless. If you give it some thought, you will come up with something that works great. Take the time to write your questions down. Using them at just the right moment will increase your sales and make the sales process much more effortless. Here is an example of a customer dialog:

Hi, Joyce, it's so nice to meet you. Thanks for asking me what I do. My specialty is to help women dramatically increase their income by creating a product suite they love. Most of my clients have discovered when they do this they start attracting their ideal client who is eager to pay them what they want. I care so much about helping women find their deepest level of clarity because I don't want anyone else to struggle like I did. Have you ever felt that if you could get clear it would make a big difference in your business?

Or you might ask:

Do your customers instantly "get" your product suite, or do you find yourself having to explain it?

Or another way:

I know many of my customers have struggled with getting to that level of clarity they need to create a product suite that excites them. Do you feel like you are as clear as you would like to be? Or, do you think your product suite represents the best you have to offer?

See how I used the question to ask if she had ever had the same experience as my customers and me? A probing question like that is designed to entice the other person into giving you information. It also creates a memorable connection with you while allowing them to open up and hear you. Their answer prompts what to say next. Ask open-ended questions that don't require yes or no answers. The other thing to note is that these sentences were crafted so my listener can tell I know what I am talking about. It gives me credibility and tells the listener why I care about helping my customers. Craft your questions so you highlight your knowledge and expertise. Be friendly and make it safe for the other person to speak freely. Now that you know how to make your pitch compelling and irresistible, let's construct your normal and natural conversation starters.

Normal and Natural Conversation Starters

Entrepreneurs tell me they loathe the selling process and would rather stick a needle in their eye than do it. Two things create this feeling. First, most people think selling is about being manipulative, and nothing is further from the truth. Second, most people don't know how to open a conversation. So they avoid it, leaving precious money on the table and missing an opportunity to be of service.

I want to point out that you start conversations all the time. As soon as there is something at stake like making money, though, you shut down and forget all of your social skills. Selling is a conversation. Talking to people about your products and services is normal. Starting a conversation with someone for sincere reasons is natural. Tap into that reserve of social grace I know you have and use it. It's part of being fully present when in the company of a potential customer. This applies in social media, email, and any other type of correspondence.

There are five normal and natural ways to start a conversation. Always respect the other person and act appropriately for the setting. Pay attention throughout your day to how easily you start conversations with others about most anything. The fact is you already know how to start a conversation effectively. Now we are going to take that skill and make it work for you when you are engaged in the sales process.

On the next page you will find five ways to start a normal and natural conversation. They include examples so you can see them in action. Practice a few times and remember customers want what you are selling or they wouldn't be talking to you.

You just never know when your biggest customer may be standing right in front of you.

There are so many ways to get a conversation started, and these five work well for most people. You can also combine any of them. Make sure to find the one that feels right to you. What matters most is that the way in which you ask is authentic, heartfelt, and genuine. Your listener will immediately warm up to you. You just never

Five Normal and Natural Conversation Starters

1. *Turn a compliment into a question.*

    Example 1: Wow, I really like they way you said that, and it seems like you have a great grasp of your niche. Do you think your product suite reflects that clarity and is helping you make the most money you could?

    Example 2: That suit you are wearing is stunning. Have you ever wanted a custom necklace that would show people you are super successful?

2. *Use the "I'm curious" statement to open a conversation. Sometimes it helps if you incorporate an observation in your statement.*

    Example 1: I'm really curious if you have ever thought about what it would take to get your business to the next level.

    Example 2: I notice you have tons of loyal followers. Does the time you spend on social media pay you back?

3. *One of my favorites is the "help me understand something" question. I am curious by nature, so this question always comes off as genuine when I ask it. This is a great way to clarify something when someone contradicts themself. It allows you to put the burden on yourself while clearing up any confusion.*

    Example: Help me understand something: I see you have a beautiful website and have written a book, so I am scratching my head wondering how it is that you aren't getting all the clients you want. Do you think your product suite isn't quite hitting the mark?

4. *Another way to get the conversation going is to comment about something you notice without asking a question. People don't like silence, so if you wait three seconds after commenting, they will most likely start talking.*

    Example: I notice you have tons of fans and followers on Facebook. You must have more customers than you can handle. [Stop and listen.]

5. *And, finally, the obvious, "Can I ask you something?" or "Can I ask you a personal question?" This is a great way to start a conversation if you think someone has a secret to something and you want to know what it is.*

    Example 1: Can I ask you something? It seems you have enjoyed tremendous success with your book. I would assume you have more clients than you can handle—how do you choose which ones to work with?

    Example 2: Can I ask you a personal question? You have written a tremendously popular book and I see your posts all over social media. What would someone as successful as you be looking for from a conference like this?

know when your biggest customer may be standing right in front of you. Rarely do you get a second chance to win them over, so use all your secret weapons. Be willing to lead a conversation and you will not only develop many new friends and acquaintances, you will surely win much more business.

With that said, there is one sale you have to make before any others, and that is with yourself.

Sell Yourself First

Can I just come right out and say it? Declare your right to be audacious! By audacious I don't mean superior or with a sense of entitlement. I mean presenting yourself, your products and services, and your pitch as though you wholeheartedly believe it. It is about feeling confident, down to your toes, in the value and worth you offer those who opt to do business with you. It is what I fondly refer to as self-sourced empowerment.

You get your tenacity and your assuredness from inside yourself. Don't apologize for promoting yourself or talking about the immense benefit your products and services provide. There is no validation big enough or meaningful enough from other people that would ever appease your need for it. Only you can give that to yourself. Let me say it again, only you can give that to yourself.

I remember back in my days in Corporate America. I thought the more I sold and the more revenue I brought in, the more I would be acknowledged by my managers. Sure, I got a few pats on the back, but from their perspective, any acknowledgement of my gifted abilities was reflected in my commission check. I longed for my managers to call me out, give me special prizes and tell me over and over how truly valuable I was. I was looking for them to nurture me on the inside. What a huge responsibility to put on someone else! It also assumes that I'm not good enough to validate myself, so the cycle perpetuates and the need gets bigger.

I was looking for that celebratory recognition that would make me feel better about myself and about being in sales. I thought I was doing something *to* my clients instead of doing something *for* my clients. Once I made the mind shift and understood the expensive and emotionally taxing problems I helped solve, I no longer needed external validation. You see, the money isn't enough. It can never make you feel good on the inside. Only your belief in doing the right thing by your customers and helping them get what they want will make you feel good. But you have to be willing to acknowledge yourself for your greatness and claim it. You have to sell yourself first so you can convince others it is right for them. After all, how can you be convincing if you aren't convinced?

Today's world is too energetically sensitive for you to be anything but real and truthful. Customers, especially female customers, can smell dishonesty and inauthenticity a mile away. Don't let your lack of faith in your greatness stop you from being irresistible to your customers. When your heart needs a hug, or you need someone to tell you that you did an awesome job, you must rely on yourself to do that. Keep track of all of your achievements, big or small, and acknowledge yourself every night before you go to bed. I bet you will find you accomplished more than you thought and were able to help so many people it was staggering. Decide right now to acknowledge your innate greatness and it will create an aura of prosperity around you!

Exercises

1. Write out your quick pitch in at least three versions using the five components.
2. Come up with at least three questions you could incorporate into your quick pitch. Practice them so that when a spontaneous opportunity arises, you know exactly what to say.
3. Write out at least one natural conversation starter using each of the three ways listed above. Play with them and start using them. Notice if one feels better than another.
4. Get a package of colorful index cards. Preferably 4 x 6. Each day, date a new card at the top. As you go through your day, jot down

what you accomplished, what hurdles you overcame, or any-thing you thought was a win. Before you go to bed each night, review the card and say out loud, "I acknowledge myself for _____." Fill in the blank for each statement you wrote on the card. If you don't have anything, acknowledge yourself for doing the best you could.

6

step four: socialize your message

IT'S TIME TO SWITCH GEARS and talk about how to generate leads using social media. As you know, social media is an amazing tool and it has leveled the playing field for everyone. It's free advertising with the benefit of conversing directly with your potential customers. However, it can be time consuming and can cost you money if you don't use it effectively. In step four, you will learn how to use social media to attract new customers without coming across as aggressive and how to turn those relationships into cash without using over-the-top promotional tactics.

Social media gives you a significant advantage to reach new customers, but you have to understand how to use it as a lead generation tool. You cannot rely on it alone to make sales. There are a few conditions, however, where you might not have to get personally involved in making the sale, such as if you are well-known or are selling something low-risk and inexpensive. Otherwise, your customers will want your personal touch to let them know you can be trusted to deliver on your promises.

One of the misconceptions about social media is that you can close deals or win business just by being active. And that you can fill a class or sell expensive goods without having to speak with your customers. Sure, it's possible, but it's not probable.

Because so many people have jumped into using social media as their primary sales tool, it is becoming harder to earn what you want from the time you spend using it. Social media can definitely help you grow your business, but you also have to understand the nuances of the landscape to make it work most efficiently for you.

Stepping Up and Standing Out

At the time of the writing of this book, the use of social media and growth of new users is at an all-time high. In fact, the largest group of people signing up for new social media accounts is those over age 45. That is exciting, because it expands everyone's customer base. It also poses a problem. The more people there are to reach, the more messages there are circulating. In other words, your efforts are now diluted because your customer has to sift through it all. The social landscape has become boisterous and noisy, not to mention confusing.

As the social web continues to grow in popularity and the volume increases, customers are becoming more conscious about who they want to do business with. They have become tired of the outrageous marketing campaigns and the demand on them to decipher sales messages. Increasingly, customers are wary of promotional Internet marketing tactics. Promotional messages are a one-way street, and they are about the seller. The power of social media is keeping it social and crafting messages that make promotion a two-way street. Customers find it refreshing and respond well. Anything else is a turn-off.

Thankfully the brazen marketing tactics and over-the-top sales promotions are fizzling out, which means you don't have to become something you aren't to win business. Nor do you have to diminish your brand by behaving in ways that don't feel right. What a relief, huh?

Step Four: Socialize Your Message

The way to win business using social media is to integrate a few important strategies. First, know that just being active won't close sales. It can create tremendous interest in what you are doing and get people to check out your products and services more closely, but the fact that you have fans, followers, and listeners isn't enough of a sales strategy on its own.

Second, start conversations with your customers in real time. You get the opportunity to provide value, showcase your expertise, and create demand. Even more exciting is the fact that others are watching, listening, and reading your exchanges. There is a positive, invisible effect on those who are listening and watching but not interacting. They get to see for themselves what you stand for and how they can benefit by doing business with you. It is called the "witnessing factor." Have you had someone reach out to you and tell you they have been following you and love what you are about? This is a huge advantage that wasn't readily available before social media. And your social behavior can turn the witnessing factor into sales. A significant portion of my private clients has come from those watching me but not commenting!

> **Your sweet spot defines your distinction.**

Third, standing out and doing it effectively is the ultimate social media challenge. The sweet spot and unique payoff proposition you defined in Step Two is the essence of your brand. Combined, those two statements represent everything you stand for. They tell the world how you differentiate what you do. Your sweet spot defines your distinction. Use every social opportunity to express it, share it and use it. You can even include it in you Twitter or Facebook bios.

Finally, the rise in popularity of social media has created a personal relationship renaissance. Your customers may have found you on social media, but now that they are familiar with you and interested in what you offer, they want to get closer. They want to talk to you. They want to ask questions and find out exactly how you can help them and at what cost. The lead you generated via social media has now become an active prospect. If you engage with them graciously, using the right social selling style, you will have taken a big step forward in realizing that lavish payback you want from your social media efforts.

More than ever, it pays to consider how you behave. Your new customers are watching. Every action you take and every post you write on social media becomes a statement about your social persona and identity as a business owner. Admit it, you are on social media to be involved in the vibrant atmosphere of entrepreneurs doing business together. You are also there because you want to make money by helping others.

Public Versus Private Selling

With the emergence of social media, two different categories of selling have been birthed: public selling and private selling. Public, or social, selling is defined as the way you handle yourself and your customer relationships on the public stage. Social selling is the beginning stages of the sales process where customers get to know you casually and learn what you do. They get to experience you as a person.

Private, or personal, selling is the second half of the sales process, in which a customer wants to speak with you in person and you have the opportunity to secure them as a paying customer. You will know you have entered into this phase when your conversation with your new customer is no longer appropriate online, in the public forum. When an interested party starts to become serious about considering your products or services, you will want to invite them to take that conversation offline. That is when you transition from public selling into private selling. The sales process becomes personalized between you and the customer. Don't worry about how to do that for now. The next two chapters will describe in detail exactly what you need to do at that stage to close the deal.

Selling socially is an art. It's one of the most powerful tools you have to create a robust customer base. The tricky part is to make sure your posts, attitude, and value fit your brand and social style. Your behavior online tells customers a lot about you. To ensure that your social media posts enhance your brand and products and services, adopt a social selling style that works for you and feels authentic to your customers.

Social Selling Styles

As social media burst open, I have noticed that some tactics work and some don't. Those entrepreneurs who gained ground rapidly while others fumbled all shared common habits. From my observations, I developed five social selling styles that run the gamut from the most to least effective. Two styles produce consistently lucrative results, one style repels customers and the remaining two don't have much effect at all.

You might see yourself in any one of these styles. Pick the one you want to become, and start using that style's effective strategies to turn your social media efforts into real, solid leads that translate into income. If you already excel at producing phenomenal results on social media, see if you can find something new in these descriptions to try.

Style #1 Ghosting

This entrepreneur posts inconsistently and uses automated tools frequently. There is no human element or "realness" to her messages, and she uses social media because she thinks she has to. This public selling style typically gets poor results because customers can sense she really isn't there.

Style #2 Posting and Coasting

This entrepreneur repeats one type of message over and over. She uses other people's material, such as quotes, re-tweets and links to other people's blogs and articles, but she doesn't share much about herself. The entrepreneur using this style probably feels overwhelmed by the social web and is struggling to define her specialty. It doesn't work well because she lacks a well-defined sweet spot and her messaging doesn't stand out.

Style #3 Boasting

This entrepreneur makes outlandish claims and talks about herself incessantly. She is concerned about making fast money and promoting herself. This style can produce results for a while, but boasters can quickly fall out of favor. This style produces unpredictable results and customers usually fade away once they notice how little this entrepreneur cares about them.

Style #4 Hosting

This entrepreneur understands that her job is to serve others first and continually provide value. She hosts events, chats, and conversations. She provides valuable guidance to her audience. She's an expert and a leader in her niche, and she generously shares what she knows with her audience. Her social conduct reflects her core values.

Have you ever been at a party where your host makes sure you have everything you need ... before you even know you need it? She offers a unique experience with great food, a great atmosphere, and great conversation that fill you up in more ways than one. You often don't want to leave. Or you leave hoping she has another party ... soon. This is the feeling that hosting can create online.

Hosting tends to produce great results because potential customers feel cared for by the host. They trust her. When a potential customer finds this type of entrepreneur via social media, they want more. They visit her site. Attend her events. Engage in a conversation with her by commenting on her blog or Facebook page or re-tweeting her tweets. And they look for more opportunities to connect.

This style tends to produce great results because potential customers feel cared for and trust the host. A host dramatically improves her results by personalizing their her message, sharing personal stories, and talking about her sweet spot more often.

Style #5 Toasting

The entrepreneur that uses this selling style is the most effective, and she produces extraordinary results. Toasting combines the traits of the Hosting style with a well-defined social persona and easily distinguishable sweet spot. (Follow Lisa Steadman on Facebook and see what I mean.)

Your social persona is the feeling, emotion, energy, words, messaging, and heart of who you are and what you're here to do. The entrepreneur who uses Toasting has developed a well-known social personality. They have the kind of persona that energizes you as well as those around you, creating the ultimate buzz and an enthusiastic and passionate following.

This entrepreneur is an influencer and people listen to her. She has the ability to effectively merge her personal and business life in a way that creates profound messages. She also is the voice of her customers' struggles, and they gravitate to her because they know she "gets it."

Toasting is an effective social selling style. It removes barriers to closing sales because this entrepreneur is highly valued and well liked. She is authentic to herself, her brand, and her mission. Everything she does is in alignment with her core values and her customers want that too. In addition, many of her followers feel as though they know her. She's a trusted friend, so they find it easy to buy from her.

The entrepreneur who uses the Toasting style celebrates her wins by drawing you into her experience. Her audience feels invested in her success and willingly spreads the word about her.

• • •

After seeing the social selling style descriptions, it should become obvious which you are and which one you want to become. The main thing with social selling is to keep it social. Be fun, lively, and engaging. Open up a bit and share the wonderful parts of your life with others, as it is appropriate for your brand. (Of course, always be safe and avoid giving away confidential information.) Use your specialty or expertise to anticipate what your customers might be thinking about. Write posts that demonstrate that you have experienced the same things they have. Ask questions in your posts to engage your followers and get them talking. Initiate the conversation.

Think of times when you were perusing your Facebook newsfeed and someone made a comment about something you were thinking but didn't want to say. All of a sudden, you feel relieved because someone else was feeling the same way and brought the subject up. Then a dialog ensues as you and others start posting back and forth about the topic. You would never have brought it up yourself but you were glad someone else did. Your customers feel the same way and love it when you make it safe for them to discuss topics in a public forum. Use discretion as is appropriate for your customers and the topic.

Here is one of my favorite examples: I used to host a Facebook fan page called Soul-O-Preneurs. One day I created a post asking the fans what they needed to do that week to dramatically increase their income. One person commented about how she had to make cold calls and hated doing so. She went on to say she avoided doing it, which was costing her money, but she knew she had to do it. Perfect opportunity! I jumped back in and politely referred her to a blog post I had written about how to "nix cold calling." I asked her to read it and let me know what she thought.

A few hours later, she reposted that the blog was exactly what she needed to start enjoying the process of calling prospective customers. She had learned a new formula for making cold calls. A couple of days later she posted that the formula had worked, and she had made sales! Can you see how powerful this is? Not only did she ask a question I could help her solve, but she just gave me an instant testimonial about providing great value that translated into money. I was hosting a conversation and she jumped in prompted by the question in my post. I provided her with a solution to her challenge, and she provided me with social proof that my techniques worked! Even better was the fact that those who were watching, but remaining invisible, witnessed this happen as well. Do you think this left a few people with a great impression of me?

You can do exactly the same thing. It feels so much better to start conversations and get your customers involved than it does to go out and promote shamelessly. Promotion is uncomfortable because it is about you and not about the customers. Yes, you have to promote yourself, but there are ways to do it that distinguish you from the crowd and include your customers in the conversation.

These new, fresh ways to behave on social media add value, strengthen your brand, and increase sales. The goal is to make this easy so the time you spend on social media translates into monetary results. To make it easy for you to get started, here are the highly effective habits of the Hoster and Toaster selling styles.

Five Effective Habits of the Hoster

Habit #1

Hosters think of their clients before themselves. They have the ability to get inside their clients' heads, and they understand their pain points as well as the results they desire. If you don't feel you fully understand your clients, ask them what they want. Create a quick five-question survey and post it everywhere. Or talk to former customers.

Sample post: "Do you want to look younger in less than a minute a day?" (It's more effective than "Feel Free Facial Serum reduces fine lines over time.")

Habit #2

Hosters start a daily dialog with customers. They relate to their customers experience or desires. They tell on themselves, making it safe for others to share their trials and tribulations, thus opening honest dialog.

Sample post: "Do you ever feel your business is growing faster than you can handle? Me too. I just noticed I was feeling that way and referred back to a chapter from my ebook about how to get unstuck. Thought I would share my favorite tip with you."

Habit #3

Once the dialog with customers is open, Hosters message back in a way to keep others talking or opening up more. Once the customer admits challenges or insecurities, the Hoster saves the day by giving advice, posting a link to a helpful blog, or creating an offer that alleviates the suffering.

Sample response: @Christina ... thank you for being so open. I hated cold calling too, until I figured out another way to do it. If it interests you, here is a link to a blog that might help.

Habit #4

Hosters watch their use of "I" and "my" in their posts and don't use them in the first sentence. They use "you," "we," or "they." Hosters are conscious of providing value, being of service, and helping in tangible ways.

Sample post: Isn't it funny that the content we teach is the content we most often need to learn? Came across this tip sheet from last year and just revised it. Amazing to see the new material was exactly what was needed. What do you think?

Habit #5

Hosters have a sixth sense about their customers and know exactly when a conversation should be taken offline. They invite their customers via email or private messaging to take the conversation to the next level. Hosters are sensitive to their customers needs and do all they can to help them without taking responsibility for them.

Sample post: @Debbie ... I hear you and can tell this is something bigger than we can handle here. I am going to send you a personal message and we can talk about some options for you. Sound good?

After you use these habits for a while, you can build on your success and work toward becoming the Toaster style. If you already have a well-developed social persona and message, then feel free to skip ahead and use the Toaster habits. It doesn't matter where you start. It matters that you learn how to use the social forum in a way that enhances sales and doesn't repel new customers.

Five Effective Habits of the Toaster

Habit #1

She blends aspects of her personal life with her business life and celebrates it in her posts. She gives people a peek "behind the curtain," sharing her life. When she does this, her audience gets to know her and like her, and she becomes a trusted friend.

> *Sample post: Sienna has learned how to hug! Have you ever been hugged by a baby? It is the most healing and wonderful feeling in the world.*

Habit #2

She focuses on the up-levels she and her clients make, celebrating and sharing those moments. The Toaster isn't afraid to acknowledge her own achievements because she does it in a way that highlights their value and not her gain. And she's not just concerned with her own success. She's genuinely happy when those around her are making strides, reaching their goals and growing, and she celebrates those as loud or louder than her own.

> *Sample post: Wow! Just ended a session with the fabulous Darcy. She's building a business based on TRUST! How does that grab you? Refreshing, I say!*

Habit #3

She uses all forms of media to express her message. She blogs and vlogs. She's a frequent guest on radio shows and podcasts. And she's a sought-after speaker. In other words, she's everywhere. She accomplishes this because she has a well-defined social persona.

> *Sample Post: Just finished speaking at the Spark & Hustle Conference and realized so many people didn't know how to develop their personal brand. Here is a video clip that might help. Would love to hear what part spoke to you.*

Habit #4

She generously gives away valuable content to help others. When you visit her website, you find an abundance of free resources. She's eager to share her knowledge. By sharing her knowledge freely, her customers are more apt to want to engage with her on a closer, personal level. They enroll in her classes and seminars. They purchase her products. And they book coaching sessions with her. They want her wisdom to shine directly on them.

> *Sample post: Celebrate! Just finished a rockin' session with @socialmediafriend and she walked away with a new biz model and started earning more cash immediately. You can do it too! Check out this free ebook with fast, fun, and friendly tips today.*

Habit #5

She posts often, is positive, and is always having fun. If she's having a bad day, we don't know it. Happiness is contagious, and she feels it's her job to help lift up others.

> *Sample post: Just met the fabulous Shirley, who came up and gave me a big hug saying, "You're the Woohoo Woman from Facebook!"*

Transitioning from Social to Private Selling

These tricks and techniques keep the gracious part of engaging intact. Your customers will notice something inspiring about you. They will be attracted to the real you and love that you don't use the same Internet marketing tactics as everyone else. It's your business and brand; behave like you care what your customers think.

The last thing to say about public or social selling is there is a natural transition point, or you can create one, when advancing the sales process with a new customer makes sense. After people have watched you for a time and decide to join in the grand conversation you are leading, they will want to get closer to you. Watch for people who become more vocal; they have realized you can help them resolve their challenge. They will make themselves known to you, and this is an indication that they might be interested in doing business with you. Start to recognize when that happens. Pay attention to someone who starts hanging around a little more closely. See if you can sense what help they could use from you and give it to them. Then invite them to schedule a time to talk to clarify their needs and readiness to buy.

When you see someone moving closer to you, becoming more involved, asking questions, or needing something more, consider these actions the early stages of a buy signal. Your social media contact has become a warm lead and by engaging with them graciously, you can move them along in the sales process. This is that natural moment when taking the conversation offline or making it personal and private will be appreciated.

Message them directly or ask them to contact you. This is a crucial point in the relationship, the point at which you will want to make them feel comfortable and welcome. You could say something like, "I notice you seem to be interested in _____. I would love to find a way to help you get what you want. Would you be willing to talk offline?" Or you could say, "I saw your post stating that you were looking for help doing _____. Don't know if you knew, but that is my specialty. What do you think about setting up a time to chat? It would be my pleasure to see if I could help you, and there is no obligation on your part."

At the beginning of this chapter we talked about the relationship renaissance. Customers are tired of being messaged repeatedly. People have forgotten how to build lasting and profitable relationships with their customers. If you take the extra step and gently invite those who are interested to learn more, you will sell more. Period. Your competitors won't do this, which gives you another distinct advantage.

Building consistent cash flow and life-long affluence will happen the more you build true and authentic relationships with people. Take the leadership role with your followers and ask them to take a closer look. They will thank you for it. Always be gracious and invitational. Transitioning your prospective customers from a social relationship to a private interaction with you will mean the difference between just paying the bills and making all you'll ever need.

Now that you are about to have a private encounter with your new customer, you will want to engage graciously so you know exactly how to turn that conversation into an eager-to-pay-you customer. Let's take a look at how you can do just that.

Exercises

1. Find three to four people you think do an excellent job of invoking conversations in social media. Take a screen shot of some of their posts and write one for yourself using theirs as an example.
2. Decide if you want to be a Hoster or a Toaster. Adopt the effective habits and start using them immediately. In fact, don't start reading the next chapter until you do!
3. You and I both know there are customers wanting to do business with you who may have not reached out. Identify two to three people who have been "hanging around" and invite them to have an offline conversation. Use it to get to know them and find out more about the kind of help they need.

7

step five:
engage graciously

I CAN'T SAY ENOUGH ABOUT how important it is to engage your customers graciously. Treating them with respect, honesty, and warmth
will make the selling process more enjoyable, fun, and delightful. Engaging your customer is important because you are deepening your
relationship and discovering if their needs match your offer. It's the
phase of the decision-making process where the customer is interested but not yet ready to buy.

The conversation between you and the customer is becoming
more personal as they disclose more intimate details about the challenge they would like resolved. Your job is to listen intently so you
know how to advise them. As the leader of the relationship, you are
in charge of guiding the conversation and providing the necessary information to help them determine their best option. Make no mistake, your customer is taking note of the manner in which you
handle the delicate balance of this new relationship. It's vital that you
provide a safe and comfortable environment for the relationship to
organically unfold.

Of course, you're polite and use your social graces. Keep doing that. What I am talking about here is expressing gratitude to your customers for the opportunity to help them. In addition, the elegant way in which you engage them lets them know what it is like to work with you. Your behavior, tone, and communication style give off cues that keep them moving forward with you. It goes beyond being nice, friendly, and polite; engaging graciously is about showing your customers you're there to serve their needs. And how you do that allows them to have an energetic experience of you, leaving an energetic imprint they can remember.

As customers get to know you and interact with you, they become familiar with how you operate. That helps them move from the interested stage into the ready-to-buy stage. Every step you take with a new customer moves them closer to or further away from buying from you. Staying true to the emotional spirit of your brand makes your customer's buying decision easier.

Think about what experience you want your customers to have when they interact with you. What would you like them to say about you? She is smart? Caring? Warm? Fun? Playful? Spunky? Powerful? She gets it? When customers, especially female customers, feel something positive from you, it increases the likelihood that they will choose your offer. The more you can express your message, style, and brand through your actions, the more effortless it will be for your customer to say yes!

Every step you take with a new customer moves them closer or further away from buying from you.

What qualities or characteristics describe you and how you interact with customers? Make a list of four to five things and post it where you can see it. Keep checking in with yourself to see if your social media posts, emails, newsletters, promotions, and conversations reflect those core values. If they do, you will be a living example of your brand. My dear friend, author and business coach Lisa Steadman, calls it "mastering your social persona." When you do that, you shorten the selling cycle and increase your ability to win business effortlessly.

For example, if you have a fun product or service, then you will want to be fun and playful during your interactions. If you service those with serious or life-threatening challenges, then you will want to let them know you are warm, discerning, and delicate. Think about if the shoe was on the other foot. How would you like to feel when talking to someone who does what you do? What qualities do your ideal customers look for?

Do you need to make customers feel safe? Do they need to see how intelligent you are? Would they be looking for you to be lively? Or warm? Maybe more serious? Based on your expertise and the nature of what you are selling, what qualities would be important to demonstrate to your customers? Integrate those into your style and you will have a wining formula.

Engaging graciously is a conscious way of being. If you act in alignment with your message, your authenticity will naturally shine through. The vibe you give off or your energetic wave is a big part of the visceral reaction a customer can have to you. I don't think enough people pay attention to this aspect of the selling process. It makes good sense that your strategy of communicating, follow-up and interacting with your customers should give customers the impression that you care. Even more so, that you are living what you are selling.

> **The vibe you give off or your energetic wave is a big part of the visceral reaction a customer can have to you.**

For example, let's say you are a spiritual life coach and someone contacts you to find out more about your services. You are rushed and respond in a cold and clipped manner. That interaction wouldn't demonstrate your spiritual tendencies. Immediately, the customer would feel that something wasn't right, and they would probably move on. Your behavior can negatively impact the customer, making it harder for you to win the business. Like it or not, customers are always evaluating your every move, and until they have worked with you and know you well, you can lose sales by not being true to the essence of your brand.

Let's look at another example. Imagine you sell organic body products and you claim your line is entirely green. But when a customer visits your website, they see that you don't use sustainable packaging. Your customer is probably going to be offended and not want to buy from you because you are clearly not walking your talk. It's astounding how sensitive a customer's radar can be, and how easily they will notice a lack in continuity between your message and your actions. Be mindful of your customers' antennae by always expressing your core values.

Simply put, gracious engagement is about leading by example and showing your customers you live what you preach. It's a measure of authenticity customers are looking to find from you. If the way you act does not match your brand, then you diminish and tarnish the customer's perception. That isn't prudent, nor is it profitable!

To ensure that you always engage graciously, write down five phrases you would like to have said about you. Include the four to five qualities you identified earlier. Write a gracious engagement creed and live by it. These words and phrases should be reflected in your every action, making it clear to your customers that you are genuine. If you have a staff, share this creed with them and make su re they stand by and uphold it.

Another thing customers carefully assess is the human element. Social media changed the need to present a perfect package. Customers respond more to truth, honesty, and transparency. They want to hear how you've used your products or services to help yourself and others. They want to relate to you and feel some type of connection. What you say and how you say it is the fastest way to build that rapport with them. Tell on yourself, tell your story, share customers' stories appropriately, and let people know the real you. They crave that and will respond eagerly to you.

Customers respond more to truth, honesty and transparency.

As you engage with your customers, there is another skill that is vitally important to master. Knowing how to listen intuitively will dramatically improve your interactions and make it easier to know what to say. Listening intuitively takes the idea of engaging graciously to a whole new level.

I remember when I first started in sales many years ago. I thought the more I talked, the more I could convince someone to buy what I was selling. If I was bright, funny, and engaging, they would see how great I was and buy from me because of it. I learned the hard way that charm doesn't sell much for long. People want to know how they will benefit. While attending the University of Santa Monica, I learned an incredibly powerful skill called heart-centered listening, and it has made all the difference in my sales ability. It taught me how to listen intuitively to my customers, and it is one of my secret weapons to selling effortlessly. It involves hearing what the customer is saying and not saying; the inaudible information allows for the most powerful interactions.

In Ron and Mary Hulnick's book, *Loyalty to the Soul,* they describe this powerful ability very well. "Really good communicators know that they will be more effective if they focus on listening to another rather than getting their point of view across. If you want to have deeper, more meaningful relationships, develop your listening skills. People yearn to be truly heard, to be received … when a person feels heard, he or she also feels loved."

Mastering Intuitive Listening

One of the ways to provide your customers with tremendous value is to listen to them closely. To actually hear what they're saying as well as what they're expressing on all levels. Creating instant rapport is easy when someone feels that they are being heard because, as the Hulnicks say, they feel loved.

The ability to listen intuitively will dramatically increase your ability to help others. It isn't that hard to do, but it requires you to be fully present and clear-headed. After a little practice, you should be able to flip a switch at a moment's notice and move into your intuitive listening mode.

Listening intuitively means you have no internal dialog running in your head. Your full attention is on your customer; you are hearing their words as well as the deeper truth beneath what they're telling you. You can feel their challenge, and when you are really dialed in, you can finish their sentences. You process the information on an energetic level and intuitively know how to handle the situation.

It's amazing how quickly this process can run its course inside of you. I like to think of it as my internal human processor, which outputs pertinent data. Something magical happens between you and your customer when you can do this. As you open up your internal channels to hear them more clearly, you move into a higher realm together. Typically you will take the customer with you and, before long, a strong alliance will be forged.

Imagine using your heart as your ears. Focus all of your attention on your customer. Forget your own worries for the few minutes you engage with your customer. Give them the gift of your precious attention, and they will feel special. Your customer will feel connected to you, which triggers a gut reaction that says, "I want to work with her."

When you operate from this higher realm of listening, you automatically know what to do and say. It's the falter-free method of engaging with your customers, keeping your confidence intact and serving them to the best of your ability. And it's the secret ingredient to being successful at effortless selling.

I'm often asked how to know if you are doing it, and I believe there are two indicators. First, intuitive messages seem to trickle upward from the solar plexus. They have a tone that is easy to understand, and they make me feel warm or smile. Compare this with mental fears or mind thoughts that tumble downward from the brain. They feel dark and cause tension. Pay close attention to the way it works inside of you.

And second, notice if you feel a warmth between you and your customer. If she is excitedly agreeing with you, then you know you are hearing beyond her words. You are listening from a force that is greater than you, and it is doing the guiding.

The skill of intuitive listening is powerful because in truth you are accessing your divine intelligence channel. It's like tuning into a radio station. When the channel is clear, you receive guidance that has more vision than you do. It is an instantaneous divine upload with a built-in script that knows exactly what the situation requires.

The skill of intuitive listening is powerful because in truth you are accessing your divine intelligence channel.

This is why selling is being of spiritual service. As the seller, you are being called to tap into the universal wisdom and express that as the truth for your customer. The more you can do that, the more effortless and effective your selling will become. Later, when you combine your selling archetype and natural asking style with intuitive listening, you will have unlocked the secret to getting all the sales you want, without compromising your spirit!

Intuitive listening is one of the best life skills you could possess. You can use it anytime for anything. It has made all of my relationships stronger. When you master it, you will never be concerned about confidence because you will be engrossed in what your customers have to say.

If you believe that confidence is your main hurdle to selling well, master intuitive listening. Confidence comes into play when you don't know what to say. Being tuned in to your own divine guidance channel will eliminate this hurdle.

Intuitive listening is an extremely important skill, because this phase of the sales process is one of the most sacred that will transpire between you and your customer. If you are willing to clear your mind, focus your attention, and be fully present and attentive with your customers, you will experience a significant up-level in your business. There will be something about you that your customer won't find or feel from other people. Most likely they will choose to work with you!

Nix Cold Calling

One of the worst feelings in the world is the dread of having to make cold calls. No one likes it, believe me. The problem with cold calling is the word *cold*. Who wants to sign up for that, right? You probably hate when people phone solicit you, which leads to discomfort with having to do it yourself.

The other thing about cold calling that bothers me is that most people won't do it unless they have to because their bank account is dwindling. Making calls with this mindset is the exact opposite of engaging graciously. There is nothing alluring about calling customers when you feel under duress.

The good news is you can nix cold calling right now, today. There is a better way, and it's worked amazingly well for me. I got into sales only because I wanted the freedom that it promised. I had no idea I was going to get the phonebook or a stack of leads thrown at me and be told to turn a pile of papers into money.

But I dutifully made those calls, loathing the process. And so did the people who answered the phone. It is such an interruptive thing to call people and hit them up for money. Yuck! Knowing how much I hated being on the receiving end of those cold calls, I thought I was being morally corrupt doing it to other people. The few times people were receptive to my calls, it was because they were naturally friendly. They asked me questions and took a few minutes to get to know me. *Voila!* The light bulb went on. What if I reversed that formula and started a discussion that felt more familiar? It's what turned everything around, turning a cold call into a warm opportunity to help. I felt great making calls to see if I could improve someone's life.

The good news is you can nix cold calling right now, today.

Luckily, you don't have to struggle with this anymore—I give you full permission to nix cold calling. I'm going to share with you a formula that will transform your initial calls into a fun and graceful process.

First, let's reframe the whole idea of cold calling. You aren't going to call someone cold again. As an alternative, you are going to design and create an outreach program; your effort to find new customers and boost sales is now officially termed your outreach program.

Your outreach program is the first step you take in personally reaching out to new customers. The guidelines and examples I'm

The Four-Step Process

Step 1: Make a list of the top five to ten customers with whom you want to do business.

Step 2: Research them and thoroughly read their websites. Find something about them or their business with which you can relate.

Step 3: Put yourself in your potential customer's shoes. What business challenges do you think they might be having? How do you think your products or services could help them? Write down your answer.

Step 4: Use this information to craft your opening line and warm up your initial outreach. Everything you say should be about your customer and relevant to them. Tell them why you think your companies have a great synergy and then explain what you can do for them.

going to provide mostly apply to phone calls and direct emails, but you should consider social media posts as part of this program (refer to Chapter 6 for help.) I'm going to share the four-step process I perfected and found produced the best results. I have repeatedly used this to win meetings and build relationships with high-level executives. It magnetizes customers to you and elicits a response in record time ... and that sounds much better than doing it the other way, doesn't it?

I promise you if you do it this way, you will feel empowered. You might even think this is fun! The best part is that your new customer will be so impressed, they will always take your call or respond quickly to your email.

The Initial Outreach Formula

(Note: Use this formula for either a phone call or email.)

Headline or Greeting: Make sure your headline or greeting is provocative and interesting. Make it relevant and include the benefit your prospective customer will get from responding to you. Remember, you want your client to open your email or respond to your call.

Opening Statement: Craft a succinct opening statement that creates an instant bond and establishes rapport, using information from your research. Let them know you have something in common. You can tell them how your companies' philosophies match, let them know you have an idea for them, or mention you can help them save or make money. *Note:* If you are calling on the phone, do the two steps above and then ask a question from your irresistible pitch to pull them into the conversation.

Proof Statement: If possible, include an example of your work or a success story that proves you can do what you say. If this is an email, include links with a reason to click through. If you don't have a sample, tell them about another client's results, but only mention names if you have permission to do so. If you are calling on the phone, bring this up when it is appropriate in the conversation, and make sure to get an email address so you can follow-up with links to pertinent information.

Email Body Copy: If your product or service requires explanation, use bullet points so the email is easy to scan. This section should be no more than a few sentences or bullet points. Avoid trying to tell your whole story. Make one salient point and in the next sentence ask for them to take an action.

Here is a before and after example of an outreach letter I rewrote using this formula. Looking at their potential customer's site, it took less than five minutes to find the synergies between these two companies. (By the way, she got a response from the revised version the same day and was asked to white label this high-end spa's T-shirts!)

Before

Dear Spa:

We are an organic T-shirt company that has had a great deal of success in your type of business. All of our shirts are manufactured free of waste products and come in a wide variety of colors and sizes.

We would like to work with you and would like to send you some samples. Here is our website address and please let us know how you would like to proceed.

After

Dear (Name),

Your co-founder, _____, says it so well when she speaks of synchronicity in her video. She talks about being at the right place and the right time and also believes that growing means always changing. We at (company name), hold the same philosophy. We invite you to consider offering a product in your gift shop that is the right product in right place, to create synchronicity with your guests.

Think about it: your clients come to revitalize their lives and rejuvenate their spirits. They could leave renewed with a new T-shirt that reflects their learning from their stay, such as: Laugh Often, Today Matters, and Practice Peace. Not only will they be gently reminded of their renewal, but others will also notice that change and ask them where they went because they seem so different.

[Go into your offer to send them samples and product.]

We also want you to know that for each T-shirt sold, we plant a tree. Given that our goals are the same, it makes sense that we could find ways to partner beyond a business relationship and further support each others' causes.

(Name), thank you so much for your time and consideration. If you would be so kind as to respond to this note and let me know when is a good time to speak with you, we could discuss how our like-minded companies might join forces.

See the difference? Which note would you respond to? If your note is cold, the response will be, too! No matter which way you choose to execute your outreach program, remember to make it noteworthy, use your unique payoff proposition statement and give the receiver something to peak their interest. If you don't reach them or they don't respond, don't worry. It's time to use a follow-up strategy.

Follow-up Strategies That Get Results

Too many entrepreneurs put a tremendous amount of work into generating leads … but they don't follow up. This is good news for you because if you follow up, you will end up getting more business. Remember, we talked about today's customers being skeptical and cautious. Following up is one more step in the sales journey where you get to show customers you care. If you are engaging graciously, you are willing to take the extra step by reaching out again.

Following up doesn't have to be hard or time consuming. In fact, if you follow a few simple guidelines, it can be simple and efficient. As a business owner, this is a critically important step as you continue to build your reputation. That extra touch distinguishes you and gives happy customers that much more to say about you.

Simple Follow-Up Guidelines and Strategies

1. To the best of your ability, follow up within twenty-four hours, especially if it's a new lead. They will appreciate you jumping at the chance to help them.
2. Commit to establishing a follow-up ritual every day. Just like going to the gym, you have to decide you are going to change the way you follow up.
3. Create a follow-up template that includes the following information:
   - Customer name
   - Product discussed
   - Where they are in their decision process?
   - My next step
   - Follow up #1 by when?
   - Follow up #2 by when?
   - Follow up #3 by when?
   - Scheduled 3 follow ups into my calendar (Yes or no)

Four Fabulous Ways to Follow Up

I'm often asked what you should say when following up and how many attempts to make. Below are four methods, or formulas, you can use to get your creative juices flowing. I recommend following up at least three to four times if your prospect is important to your brand or could be lucrative for you. If after that many attempts you get no response, it's safe to assume it isn't the right time or the right match.

Approach #1: "I Missed You" or "Let's Chat"

This option is a friendly and casual way to get a response. You might use it when you and your customer are familiar with each other. Start by telling the other person you miss them and why you would like to schedule a time to chat or get together. It's a great first follow-up message, but don't use it too often or it will sound fake.

Approach #2: "I Have an Idea for You"

This approach is my personal favorite and I use it often. It's a great way to warm up a newly formed relationship. Customers like to know you are thinking about them. Craft a message telling them you were thinking about them and had a brainstorm you wanted to share. Tell them what that is, and they will love you for it. If you are calling and get voicemail, tell them you had an idea for them. Ask them to call you back to find out what it is. Watch as you get return phone calls quickly!

Approach #3: "Chopped Liver"

This approach should be used sparingly and only if you think you have nothing to lose. It works great if your customer has been non-responsive. Quite often it gets a response because it motivates the receiver to let you know everything is okay. Write a tongue-in-cheek message, letting them know you feel like chopped liver because they haven't responded. Use your word choice carefully to not offend. Because this approach is a tiny bit manipulative, it induces guilt on the other party and they typically respond. Used in the right circumstance, it works well.

Approach #4: "Closing the Door"

As a last resort, I love this approach. It works and gets the conversation going again. If you have a customer who is deciding whether or not to work with you and has gone into hiding, this will bring them out. When a customer has a strong desire to buy but cannot finalize their decision, they won't want you to leave. Construct your message to let them know how much you have enjoyed getting to know them, restate the benefit you know is waiting for them, and tell them you won't be bothering them anymore. It is a gracious way to end the relationship and take full responsibility for it not working out. If they want to work with you, they will respond so fast it will make you giggle. If they never respond, it wasn't the right time or fit.

4. When you follow up, always open your call or email with a bonding statement as suggested above. Each time you reach out to your customer, electronically or live, use an opening line that reminds them of the benefit or value waiting for them should they respond. This warms up your communication, easing the customer's mind. Keep in mind that every contact with your customer is an opportunity to build trust and a relationship.

5. Remember the intention of the follow up is to help your customer take the next step. Try not to use it to prematurely close the deal.

6. Take at least thirty seconds to check in intuitively and decide which approach fits the situation. You can use all of them and mix it up or use one repeatedly. Be confident in your choice.

• • •

The secret to following up is knowing when to cut bait. You can spend too much time on someone who isn't going to buy when you could be finding a new customer who is eager to pay you. Again, use your intuitive abilities to guide you. It's okay to let a customer go. If you engage with them graciously and use these tools, they will be back. It's what I know to be true and why these methods are so effective.

Now that you know how to engage graciously and behave in a way that enhances your brand, let's discover your signature selling archetype so you can turn all of your leads into cash.

Exercises

1. Make a list of the four to five words that describe your brand. Post them where you can see them.

2. Make a list of four to five phrases you would like your customers to say about you. Turn these words and phrases into a "gracious engagement" creed. Live by it, stand by it, and make sure your customers experience your core values firsthand.

3. Turn your lead-generation strategy into an outreach program. Make it official, and never say the words "cold calling" again.

4. Start practicing intuitive listening and honor what your inner guidance tells you to do.

5. Always follow up and tune in to your intuition. Pick an appropriate follow-up strategy. Keep track of how many times you follow up with someone. If it's time to let them go, do so.

8

step six: discover your signature selling archetype

ONE MORNING DURING YOGA, I had what I call a "divine download," one of those energetic experiences where a new way of doing something crystallizes before me. I'll be honest: I had been struggling writing this book. (This is the fourth version!) Something wasn't coming through.

And then there it was: Right in the middle of downward dog I realized I was trying to teach *you* how to sell like *me*. And there just wasn't any way someone without my experience, knowledge, background, and personality was going to be able to sell like me.

I initially believed you are either a natural born seller or you must reassemble yourself to become one. But I realized that notion was based on an old school way of thinking. In the entrepreneurial environment, or the "big girl" business model, you don't need to close a deal the way you do in Corporate America. It isn't about beating the competition or exceeding sales forecasts. It's about sharing your heartfelt message and solutions with your customers in a way that feels good to you, rewards you lavishly, and benefits your buyers.

And here's the best part: Under this new method, you only need to learn how to sell in a way that matches *your* personality and *your* strengths. You learn to sell like you, not like me.

You already have a natural style that convinces and influences people. It's time to translate that skill to sales. I have created a new selling paradigm just for you. Are you ready to discover your signature selling archetype? You have one that fits you perfectly. You don't have to change who you are; you just have to embrace your passion and be willing to share it.

Claim Your Signature Selling Archetype

There are twelve archetypes. One will be your dominant style, and it's possible to have a second, less dominant style. Each archetype has core strengths as well as weaknesses, or pitfalls.

Once you identify your archetype, you'll begin to see yourself as someone who is capable of selling your products and services. And when you claim your signature selling archetype fully, you'll experience such an unwavering belief in your offering that you'll exude a magnetic confidence. It's the best customer attraction model in the world!

How to Claim Your Signature Selling Archetype

1. Read the descriptions in their entirety.
2. Read them again, this time putting checkmarks next to the archetypes that resonate with you.
3. Go back and look at the archetypes you checked—which one is calling your name the loudest?
4. Try your best to narrow it down to one.
5. And, finally, avoid choosing an archetype because you think it sounds better than another; every archetype is great in its own right.

Step Six: Discover Your Signature Selling Archetype

The Twelve Signature Selling Archetypes

As you read through the archetypes, keep in mind they aren't complete personality portrayals. Instead, they're indicators for the way in which you talk about your products and services; they're a reflection of how you operate as a business owner. Each archetype also has pitfalls, which are limiting characteristics that consistently cost you money. The pitfalls aren't meant to be negative judgments, they're traits waiting to be developed into something fruitful.

When you've identified and claimed your dominant signature selling archetype, try it on for a few days. But don't worry about how to use your archetype to close business or ask for the sale. We will cover that in step seven.

Are you ready to meet the signature selling archetypes? Then turn the page, because I can't wait to introduce you to them!

The Humanitarian Archetype

The Humanitarian Archetype is compassionate and giving. She holds a wealth of knowledge and truly wants to help others learn what she knows. The Humanitarian tends to be a little shy or humble and is intimidated by anything to do with selling. She cares deeply about helping people any way she can and often takes on too much work that strays from her heart's desire. The Humanitarian would rather go out of business then ever say anything that sounds or feels "salesy."

Characteristics of the Humanitarian Archetype

Positive Traits:

- ☐ Shy, humble, soft-spoken
- ☐ Cares deeply about others
- ☐ Wants her customers to like her
- ☐ Compassionate, approachable, unselfish
- ☐ Naturally well liked
- ☐ Has a benevolent nature and is well meaning in all that she does
- ☐ Has a heart of gold

Pitfalls:

- ☐ Has a tendency to underestimate her value and worth
- ☐ Gives away too much as she is more worried about being liked than being profitable
- ☐ Avoids raising her prices because she doesn't want to offend anyone
- ☐ Spends too much time wishing for business
- ☐ Not always as motivated or ambitious as her goals would indicate

☐ This resonates with me   ☐ This is me

Biggest Selling Challenge

When the Humanitarian Archetype is faced with closing the sale, she starts to worry about offending customers for fear they won't like her, so she plays it safe, keeping her prices low and hesitating to ask for the business. She is susceptible to losing business to others who have stronger selling skills.

The Temptress Archetype

The Temptress Archetype appears goddesslike and entices customers with her story, image, or lifestyle. She uses her feminine wiles in all areas of her life. She is alluring, and she boldly asks her customers to pay top dollar. She isn't afraid of selling, but her style can be misperceived as manipulative if she isn't thoughtful in her approach.

Characteristics of the Temptress Archetype

Positive Traits:

- ☐ Empowered, seductive, alluring
- ☐ Comfortable with herself
- ☐ In tune with her customers
- ☐ Savvy in her industry
- ☐ Leads an exciting life
- ☐ Thought of as a role model
- ☐ Has an uncanny ability to attract customers
- ☐ Appears to have it all

Pitfalls:

- ☐ Her seductive nature repels some women
- ☐ Borders on being manipulative, tempting customers into buying things they may regret later
- ☐ Flip flops between being too nice or too hard, confusing her customers
- ☐ Likes to be the center of attention
- ☐ Enamored with herself and loses customers because she forgets to leave room for them to grow or shine
- ☐ Can be challenged when it comes to providing details and delivering results

☐ This resonates with me   ☐ This is me

Biggest Selling Challenge

The Temptress Archetype doesn't have a problem asking her customers to buy from her or to pay high prices. She is sure she deserves it. The trouble spot for the Temptress is in her need to feel seductive and in control. For her, the act of seducing gives her sheer pleasure. Sometimes she gets drunk on her own message and loses the sale because she's arrogant. She can forget to appeal to the customer's heart and mind by being too vague about her promises.

3

The Romantic Archetype

The Romantic Archetype is everyone's sweetheart. She is playful and is someone you want to hang out with. She is charming and easy to be with, and she has a casual type of intelligence. The Romantic Archetype lives a carefree, highly social life. She also has an idealized view of life and others, making her a little naive. She tends to count her money before she has completed the sale, and her sentimentality blinds her ability to read her customers' intentions correctly.

Characteristics of the Romantic Archetype

Positive Traits:
- ☐ Charming
- ☐ Fun, playful, easy to be with
- ☐ Makes her customers feel special
- ☐ Intelligent
- ☐ Becomes deeply involved in her customer's business
- ☐ A little bit mischievous
- ☐ Passionate about helping others
- ☐ Can quickly become a trusted friend
- ☐ Can be a little seductive, but she is too forthcoming to be the Temptress

Pitfalls:
- ☐ Believes being someone's trusted buddy is enough to close the sale
- ☐ Loathes asking for the business and thinks her courting strategies are enough to get her customers to buy
- ☐ Tends to have her head in the clouds, worrying customers about whether she can deliver on her appealing promises
- ☐ Gets sentimental and falls in love with her customers, blinding her to her customers' needs during the decision-making process
- ☐ Lacks structure and has a hard time staying focused

☐ This resonates with me   ☐ This is me

Biggest Selling Challenge

The Romantic Archetype thinks the sales process is dirty. She doesn't like how it makes her feel and prefers to "court" her customers, winning them over with pure charm. After spending time bonding with her customers, she gets frustrated that they don't plunk down their credit card without prompting from her. To avoid feeling awkward with the selling process, she makes enticing offers (leaving precious dollars on the table), thinking it will close the deal and protect her from "getting dirty" during the process.

The Maverick Archetype

The Maverick Archetype is smart, quirky, and audacious. She's a tiny bit flirty but she's also sensible. She has the uncanny ability to see more about her customers than they see about themselves. She has tons of moxie, hidden and unhidden. Mostly she's an individualist who will protect her freedom at all costs. This is where selling can get tricky for her; she will turn her back if she thinks making a sale will trap her or curtail her freedom.

Characteristics of the Maverick Archetype

Positive Traits:

- ☐ Carefree, hip, modern, mystical, and edgy
- ☐ Super smart and highly creative
- ☐ Senses change first
- ☐ Eccentric and playful
- ☐ Usually plays a leadership role
- ☐ Often mistaken for being an artist when, in fact, she has a great head on her shoulders
- ☐ Highly creative, often the life of the party
- ☐ Customers love her quirkiness
- ☐ Open and friendly yet selective of who she will work with

Pitfalls:

- ☐ Unorthodox, confusing some new customers
- ☐ Perceived as weird if she takes her quirkiness too far in the business world
- ☐ Rebellious, which can make her inflexible to some customer's needs
- ☐ Unpredictable, leaving some customers questioning if she can deliver on her promises
- ☐ Intimidating to some customers, often those who need her products and services the most

☐ This resonates with me   ☐ This is me

Biggest Selling Challenge

The Maverick Archetype struggles with sales for two primary reasons. First, selling means she has to be committed to fulfilling on a promise, and to her that means selling out. The Maverick would rather give up a sale than lose one ounce of her freedom or compromise her creativity. And second, the Maverick is so busy being free and wild, she doesn't really want to be bothered with the sales process. Yes, she wants to help her customers, but she doesn't want to spend one minute helping them decide. On the other hand, if the Maverick becomes too obvious about wanting to make a buck, she will lose her magnetic funkiness.

5

The Nurturer Archetype

The Nurturer Archetype is steadfast, warm, and supportive. She encourages her customers' growth and celebrates their accomplishments and wins. She tends to pamper her customers and takes little credit for the vast wealth of knowledge she possesses. She invests so much time, attention, and energy in her customers, they buy from her repeatedly. The Nurturer Archetype can forget to take care of herself and is prone to overextending herself on her customers' behalf.

Characteristics of the Nurturer Archetype

Positive Traits:
- [ ] Trustworthy, accomplished, and well respected
- [ ] Has a stellar reputation and earns customers' respect easily
- [ ] Intelligent, intuitive, pragmatic, and orderly
- [ ] Provides her customers with deliverables that far exceed their expectations
- [ ] Instinctively knows how to help her customers be better
- [ ] Has a keen sense of how to care for her customers without smothering them

Pitfalls:
- [ ] Has a tendency to put her customers' needs above her own
- [ ] Can promise too much and ask for too little in return
- [ ] Forgets to check in with herself and determine when it's time to take a break or rest
- [ ] Hates to say no and can easily become over-burdened with too much work
- [ ] Fails to construct a business model that factors in her need for personal balance
- [ ] Hesitates to establish boundaries because she fears losing the opportunity to help her customers

[ ] This resonates with me   [ ] This is me

Biggest Selling Challenge

The Nurturer Archetype is neutral about selling. She's happy to do it if she can find a style that is warm and caring; otherwise she won't work too hard at it. Because she has given so much by the time she gets to the point of asking for the business, she is tired, sensitive, and irritable. In some cases, the Nurturer will get sick because she forgets to pace herself. This undermines her business and profitability. In her exhaustion to develop a deep bond with her customers, she often gives up too soon. Or gives in to get the sales process over with.

The Visionary Archetype

The Visionary Archetype sees what others cannot and is usually leading a movement. She is a multi-passionate entrepreneur and tends to have her hands in many different businesses. She hardly ever looks back and rarely apologizes for her boldness. She moves quickly and knows herself to be capable of most anything. She has to be careful not to offend her customers because her rapid movement through life can be perceived as disinterest, while others are intimidated by her prowess.

Characteristics of the Visionary Archetype

Positive Traits:

- ☐ Upwardly mobile
- ☐ A massive multi-tasker
- ☐ Well educated
- ☐ Able to see far into the future and instinctively know what to do
- ☐ Smart, dynamic, imaginative, ambitious, and creative
- ☐ Rarely gets thwarted
- ☐ Shrewd, unstoppable, and extremely enterprising
- ☐ Everything she touches turns to gold
- ☐ Transparent about her struggles, endearing her to her customers

Pitfalls:

- ☐ Intimidating because she moves quickly
- ☐ Susceptible to missing out on business opportunities that are right in front of her because she is too focused on the future and on getting to where she wants to go
- ☐ Can see the future before others do, making her impatient with customers who don't "get it" quickly enough
- ☐ Has a short attention span and doesn't do well with super needy customers
- ☐ Tends to gloss over her customers' sensitivities because she is driven and decisive

☐ This resonates with me　　☐ This is me

Biggest Selling Challenge

The Visionary Archetype is wise and has much to offer; however, her short fuse and lack of patience for other people's decision-making process keep her from spending the proper time needed to close a sale. She believes helping customers make a decision is something they should do on their own, just like she does. Selling annoys her because she feels like it's holding her back from achieving her goals. Thus, she loses money because customers who want hand-holding won't get it from her.

7

The Mentor Archetype

The Mentor Archetype is well versed and experienced in her field and has tons of street credibility. She is known for blending her expansive wisdom with a nurturing quality that leaves her customers feeling well cared for. She's respected and trusted because she is the real deal. She has mastered her topic and is usually humble about her vast experience and credentials. Customers crave what she knows and clamor to work with her. The Mentor Archetype has to stay consistent and clear in her messaging or she'll appear too lofty.

Characteristics of the Mentor Archetype

Positive Traits:

- [ ] Highly intuitive, intellectual, honest, full of integrity
- [ ] Comfortable with herself and doesn't feel threatened by her customers or their growth
- [ ] Instinctually knows how to adopt her style to each customer, making it easy for customers to relate to her
- [ ] Can re-language most anything on the spot
- [ ] Is able to hear what *isn't* being said
- [ ] Pulls clever solutions seemingly out of thin air
- [ ] Is clearly the leader in her relationship with her customers
- [ ] Provides customers with tremendous value

Pitfalls:

- [ ] Can become stuck in a rut
- [ ] Needs to keep her outlook and content fresh
- [ ] Needs to allow time to properly rejuvenate
- [ ] Has to stay in-tune with her customers' words and incorporate them into her messaging to stay relevant
- [ ] Can have a short fuse or become impatient when customers take time to assimilate what they learn from her
- [ ] Is prone to taking over when the customer needs time to think
- [ ] Is prone to sounding 'preachy' and has to remember her own learning curve

[ ] This resonates with me   [ ] This is me

Biggest Selling Challenge

The Mentor has two primary selling challenges. First, she can become bored with the process and doesn't always work as hard as she could. Second, the Mentor is so steeped in her expertise, she doesn't always relate well to her customers' problems because dealing with the problem happened a long time ago for her. She needs to develop more empathy and use her intuition to correctly discern what her customers actually need from her.

The Heroine Archetype

The Heroine Archetype is a natural-born leader and today's modern warrior princess. She is known to have strong convictions and will defend her cause and her customers fiercely. She is noble in her efforts and wants to give her customers the best. She wants to save them from pain or struggle and knows how to reach into their hearts. The Heroine tends to be a rescuer as well, which means she has to watch out for customers who play the victim card.

Characteristics of the Heroine Archetype

Positive Traits:
- ☐ Loyal, courageous, noble
- ☐ Wants to relieve her customers of their burdens
- ☐ Mission driven and head strong
- ☐ Seems super human
- ☐ Performs many tasks well
- ☐ Is a fighter and is idolized by her customers
- ☐ Has made outstanding achievements; many wish to be like her or model her systems
- ☐ Respected in her leadership role
- ☐ Is easy to talk to and, depending on her industry, makes uncomfortable topics comfortable to talk about

Pitfalls:
- ☐ Can scare shy customers because of her strength and zealousness
- ☐ Can be so idolized by her followers, they're shocked if she stumbles or makes a mistake
- ☐ Is expected to be perfect and know the answer to everything all the time
- ☐ Can be a bit antagonistic and, at times, seem elitist to those who are less ferocious than she is
- ☐ Prone to growing a big ego in the name of her cause
- ☐ Needs to strike an appealing balance between serving her customers and her mission
- ☐ Tends to attract needy, high-maintenance customers

☐ This resonates with me   ☐ This is me

Biggest Selling Challenge

The Heroine Archetype assumes that demonstrating her expertise is enough to get customers to buy. She uses her ability to win on the playing field as evidence she is worthy of her customer's money. But she forgets to appeal to her customer's emotional needs while she is busy proving herself. The Heroine thinks it's beneath her to ask for the sale and would rather fall on her sword than do it.

9

The Mystic Archetype

The Mystic Archetype is spiritual first and business-oriented second. She is on a journey to spearhead a movement that is bigger than her. Her products and services support the fulfillment of her ultimate mission. She has a deep desire to connect with those who are like-minded. She seeks more than business from her customers; she is looking for unity and partnership. She is a truth-seeker and serves her higher calling by helping her customers. She feels that asking for money is impure, taints her efforts, and clouds her vision.

Characteristics of the Mystic Archetype

Positive Traits:

- ☐ Is attuned to her inner spiritual purpose
- ☐ Easily attracts and bonds with her customers
- ☐ Is intelligent, organized, and driven by a need to fulfill her mission
- ☐ Is highly intuitive
- ☐ Creates deep, meaningful, and lasting bonds with her customers
- ☐ Is great at enrolling others in her vision
- ☐ Develops products and services that are exceedingly desirable
- ☐ Is tremendously gifted and wants others to experience the bliss she does
- ☐ Knows having a successful and profitable business supports her cause (and that is what keeps her going)

Pitfalls:

- ☐ Can be perceived as flighty when in fact she is serious about her business
- ☐ Can become obsessed about her cause and develop a righteous attitude
- ☐ Can be misunderstood or considered ungrounded
- ☐ Seems too optimistic, which positions her as mysterious
- ☐ Has a tendency to rely solely on the strength of her mission to generate money instead of providing customers with concrete benefits

☐ This resonates with me   ☐ This is me

Biggest Selling Challenge

The biggest selling challenge for the Mystic is her attitude. She considers herself to be naturally abundant (and she is); however, she thinks asking for money is impure. She views herself as someone who doesn't have to ask for money but will manifest it instead. She is motivated to generate money for her cause, but for her to feel good about asking for money, she has to reconcile how her products and services help her customers realize their aspirations.

The Artist Archetype

The Artist Archetype is highly creative and very smart, and she thinks making money or being in business is a necessary evil. She believes that being an artist is the most noble thing she can be, and she rejects anything she perceives as tainting her artistry. She doesn't like to talk about money and spends most of her time in a creative state.

Characteristics of the Artist Archetype

Positive Traits:

- ☐ Has unmatched flair, style, and artistic nature
- ☐ Is extremely creative, intuitive, and intelligent
- ☐ Thinks being an artist is the highest form of self-expression and prides herself on being uniquely original
- ☐ Wants to make money by getting paid well for her creative endeavors
- ☐ Can be thrifty and pragmatic as much as she can be imaginative
- ☐ Offers customized, unique products and services, giving her a significant competitive advantage

Pitfalls:

- ☐ Doesn't see the world through her customers' eyes and tends to misunderstand their emotional need for her products or services
- ☐ Can appear arrogant or aloof due to her protective, sensitive nature
- ☐ Believes she is superior to "business types" and thinks making a lavish income in her desired profession means she has sold out
- ☐ Puts high expectations on her clients because she expects a lot from herself
- ☐ Needs to add more warmth and empathy to her approach
- ☐ Struggles with messaging and brand identity because she sees creativity and imagination as boundless

☐ This resonates with me ☐ This is me

Biggest Selling Challenge

Of all the archetypes, the Artist struggles most with selling. Being involved in someone's purchasing decision makes her feel dirty and untrustworthy. Selling is loathsome for the Artist, and she avoids it. She believes her creativity is reason enough for customers to buy. She wants nothing to do with the sales process, leaving her customers feeling as though they're unimportant to her.

11

The Liberator Archetype

No matter what she does, the Liberator Archetype specializes in helping others to transform. She always knows exactly what her customers need. It's as if she can see right through them and into their higher purpose. She possesses the innate ability to boldly get her customers to open up and discuss things they don't tell many people. For some reason she was blessed with knowing how to unlock her customers' freedom. She has to be careful not to take on too many of her customers' issues, becoming overly responsible for the results they produce.

Characteristics of the Liberator Archetype

Positive Traits:

- ☐ Is keenly aware of her customers' deepest desires
- ☐ Works quickly, providing strong deliverables
- ☐ Highly trustworthy
- ☐ Can get many things done on her customers' behalf in record time
- ☐ Is almost always in the service industry and can facilitate a deep, lasting transformation in her customers
- ☐ Takes great care of her customers and illuminates their new path
- ☐ Is brave and bold in her process
- ☐ Knows how to hold the space for her customers' greatest growth

Pitfalls:

- ☐ Tends to care so much about her customers' future, she is prone to taking too much responsibility for their progress
- ☐ Underestimates the tangible value of her services
- ☐ Doesn't manage her boundaries appropriately
- ☐ Can become impatient with a client because the future is clear to her and not to them
- ☐ Switches from a serving mode into a rescuing mode and can become an enabler
- ☐ Can become overly focused on getting her customers to realize their full potential and forgets to acknowledge their progress

☐ This resonates with me ☐ This is me

Biggest Selling Challenge

The Liberator Archetype is so focused on facilitating the next transformation, she forgets to ask for the business. She is usually not afraid of selling or getting her customers to commit. Her challenge is getting paid what she deserves and being willing to ask for more. She is in the habit of giving away more than she gets, and because she loves what she does, she neglects to raise her prices.

The Sassy Savant Archetype

The Sassy Savant Archetype is gifted and intellectually talented. She does for other people what they don't want to do for themselves. She loves being the smartest girl in the room and has a tendency to be mischievous. While people are in awe of her cleverness, she also entertains her customers by letting just a little of her court jester side out. She has to be careful to not overpower others with her intellectual power and remember that she can win more business by being warm and friendly.

Characteristics of the Sassy Savant Archetype

Positive Traits:
- ☐ Willingness to share her special gifts with her customers in service to make their lives easier
- ☐ Is smart, well respected, and extremely trustworthy
- ☐ Does well what others find difficult
- ☐ Possesses a vast breadth and depth of knowledge in her field
- ☐ Is typically viewed as an expert
- ☐ Is organized and efficient, and excels at her craft
- ☐ Is clever and bright, letting her customers know they're in good hands

Pitfalls:
- ☐ Thinks she is smarter than others and can be inflexible when customers want something customized
- ☐ Forgets to be warm and friendly while she is busy proving how smart and funny she is
- ☐ Forgets to listen to her customers and empathize with their situation
- ☐ Doesn't know how to put her valuable offer in context for her customers
- ☐ Doesn't want to work too hard at solving problems that don't fit neatly into her business model

☐ This resonates with me   ☐ This is me

Biggest Selling Challenge

The Sassy Savant Archetype has the most unique position of all the archetypes: Because she is gifted in ways most others are not, she knows she has leverage over her customers. She doesn't like to sell because she thinks it's beneath her. She is convinced that her customers should easily recognize the value she provides without her having to explain it. She can miss out on making money because she fails to paint a clear enough picture of the value she provides.

Do you see yourself in any of these archetypes? Maybe more than one jumps out at you. Read through them again, this time putting a checkmark by those that resonate with you most. You can have qualities of many of the archetypes but one will fit you best. Again, this is not an ego contest. These archetypes were designed so you can own your strengths and overcome your pitfalls.

When you believe you've identified your signature selling archetype, put the book down for a few days and try her on. Like a new coat, notice if she feels good. Lean into her.

If after a few days she still feels right, start to become aware of the times you fall into the limiting aspects, or pitfalls, that are keeping you from making all you'll ever need. Becoming aware of behaviors that limit your cash flow can be confronting; however, it can also be enlightening. Use what you learn about your signature selling archetype as an opportunity for growth.

If you're not sure which archetype fits you best or if the archetype you chose doesn't fit, repeat the process. Review the list again and narrow it down to two choices. Meditate on it and ask for clarity,, and you'll know exactly which way to go.

If you are still having a hard time making a choice, ask yourself if you are unwilling to take a closer look at yourself. If you are, that is okay. Journal about it for a few days until you can freely and honestly make a choice.

Remember, you can also have a less dominant archetype, but for now, focus on your dominant style. Your signature selling archetype should feel like a familiar friend. She will guide you forward in your business. Embrace her and attune to the knowledge and wisdom she carries. Bring her into your sales conversations and watch how effortless it becomes.

It's time to take the next step toward getting the effortless yes from your customers; to graciously ask them to do business with you. You'll quickly see how what was once uncomfortable can suddenly feel right to you.

Exercises

1. Make a check mark next to the archetype that feels right.
2. Review your list and choose which archetype is your dominant archetype before you read the next chapter.
3. Take your time with this because it will be important to the results you produce using the natural asking styles.

(*Note:* It is possible you can have a dominant and non-dominant archetype. For now, just choose one.)

9

step seven: perfect your natural ask

I HOPE YOU COULDN'T WAIT to get to this chapter and are excited to discover and perfect your natural asking style! This is new information, and getting acclimated will take time. It's in your best interest to have settled on your signature selling archetype before you read this chapter so it's relevant and useful.

What is a "natural ask" and what does that mean? As you go through the sales cycle with your customer, there comes a point when it's natural for the transaction to conclude. You both will either want to do business together or not. By now you've invested time and energy in helping your customer understand how they will benefit from your product or service. There is a delicate point in the process when spending any more time, energy, or effort in educating a customer would be a loss for you. The customer doesn't want to vacillate forever either. It's important to stay alert and notice when that time comes. Naturally, the selling process has to end and the work has to begin. That is the ideal time to ask for the business.

If you don't ask the customer where they stand, they will say they need to think about it and go away. Left to their own devices, customers usually don't take action. A non-decision is a decision. It most likely means they aren't going to buy from you. This is the most costly mistake you could make. Money gets left on the table—dollars you could retire on—from neglecting to finalize the sale. It's critical to your financial success to complete the sales process side by side with your customer.

Asking the customer for their decision is a natural step during the selling process. Customers like it because it demonstrates leadership on your part and prompts them to make a final decision. It also demonstrates that you have confidence in your offering. The asking step encourages the customer to take the next step with you, agreeing to make the purchase and form a partnership. This is when the sale is made or not. Remember, making the sale or winning the business is the first step to working together. It's one big step in the overall relationship. For now, don't worry about any objections that may arise, we are going to talk about that in the next chapter.

Why is the ask so important? Not asking is absolutely the biggest mistake most people make, and even the world's best salespeople had to overcome this hurdle. Until you understand that your customer wants you to lead them to a decision, you'll feel uneasy when it comes time to close the sale. Think back to when we discussed the buyer's decision-making process and asking will make more sense now. Your customers aren't as scary as you might think. They're looking to you to support their ability to arrive at a final decision. They aren't going to bite your head off; they want something you have. They will question the validity of the relationship, if you fail to help them reach a decision.

Asking builds even more faith and trust in your relationship and products and services, beyond what you've already built. It's the last little detail that shows you care about the customer and are putting their needs first. Asking your customer helps them say yes, and they will eagerly buy from you if you do. Most of your competitors won't ask. If you do, you've gained a natural advantage.

Let's talk about "closing the sale," since this phrase can make people nervous. The majority of the selling process is telling your story, sharing the improvements your customers see when they use your products and services, and explaining what value your customers get. That isn't so awkward, right? In fact, that part is fun and gratifying. It's when it comes to asking for the business or solidifying the deal with your customer that nerves kick in. Most people don't even take this step because this is what feels dirty, "salesy," impure, and arrogant about selling.

The difference between those who make all they'll ever need and those who barely get by is the skill of asking for the business.

Now I'm going to let you in on a little secret. Scratch that; make it a BIG secret. The difference between those who make all they'll ever need and those who barely get by is the skill of asking for the business. Let me repeat: The difference between those who make all they'll ever need and those who barely get by is the skill of asking for the business.

This part of the selling process gets a bad rap because often sellers who do ask either ask for the business too early in the "getting to know you" phase or ask in a way that feels like they care more about making the sale than they do about you.

Let's redefine the asking portion. When you serve your customers generously, that includes helping them make the decision. If you don't ask them to make a decision, there is a good chance they never will. If they don't, they cannot receive the gifts of your offering. Is that what you want for your customers?

And while we're at it, let's clear something up: The term "closing the sale" was invented by Corporate America to standardize and label the end of a business transaction. It means that the transaction between two parties is complete or near completion. It isn't an attractive or fitting term in the entrepreneurial world. Big business is more neutral and less personal in nature, so terms like that work. But the entrepreneurial space is more personal and warm. It's filled with women who prefer to keep their femininity in tact. Using a term like "closing the sale" feels like there is no caring or respect for the customer. Therefore, most entrepreneurs shy away from asking.

I used to hate asking, too. Just out of college, I worked at Enterprise Rent-A-Car. We were supposed to up-sell the customer into an expensive damage waiver clause, and my manager was standing over my shoulder with his you-better-do-it-or-get-fired look. So I did it, I asked. The customer's reaction wasn't as bad as I expected, but he did say no. Relieved, I thanked him for listening. I finished renting him the car and ran back inside. My manager called me over, and I told him to wait just a second. I ran to the bathroom and threw up. I was horrified. My first thought was, "I graduated from college to do this?"

Later that afternoon, I met with my manager. I thought he was going to fire me, but instead he told me why the damage waiver was a good deal for customers. He told me why customers should consider buying it, and a light bulb went on in my head. It felt different. Instead of asking them to spend more money for the sake of pleasing my manager, I could explain how they could avoid a hassle should something happen.

It was one of my first big sales lessons. I remember my mind shifting when I realized I was being of service by giving my customer an informed choice. If I didn't tell him about the damage waiver, I was concealing important information. I could see that asking for the business was being helpful. And the secret to asking for the business is to believe wholeheartedly that what you are selling is good for the customer.

In the previous chapters, you've taken the steps to see that what you are selling is of tremendous value to your customers. By perfecting your natural ask, you'll forever increase the amount of money you make. There is no more powerful a skill you could incorporate into your business than knowing how to finesse this part of the selling conversation.

The reason I was able to develop the archetypes and their natural asks is because I have been every archetype and used every ask in my quest to sell effortlessly. Those that work best for me make me the most comfortable and influence my customers. My wish is that this will become the truth for you, too.

In the end, you get to choose which outcome you want for yourself. Do you want to learn how to ask for the business in a way that feels good to you and works? I have developed twelve natural asking styles. They all work. Use the ask that plays to your strengths and graciously ask for the business.

The Twelve Natural Asking Styles

Before I reveal the twelve natural asking styles, understand that each is paired with its primary archetype and is designed to work with those core strengths. You may find you like more than one style. The asking styles are interchangeable; you can take pieces of one and combine them with another. If you haven't been asking for the business from your customers, I suggest starting with the style associated with your dominant archetype.

Each natural asking style comes with a description, a fictional example of it in use and its most compatible archetype. I've also included a formula to prompt you to write your own version, using the words and phrases from your unique payoff proposition.

Put a checkmark next to the styles that feel good to you. Pay special attention to the styles that get you excited because those will be the ones you'll use most of the time. Remember, customers respond to enthusiasm and excitement so use that to your advantage when determining the style that best suits you. Most of the styles work well for products or services. Please read through all of them because it will spark new ideas about how you can perfect and customize your natural ask! Isn't it thrilling to know you are going to make more money so effortlessly?

1

☐ The Sympathetic Ask

This style of asking lets you relate to the concerns your customer has expressed about buying your products or services. It's one of the softer asks, but it's effective nonetheless. First, repeat your customer's concerns, which shows you empathize with them. Now take it one step further and tell them how your product or service addresses and, therefore, alleviates those concerns. The Sympathetic Ask lets you complete the transaction while you express consideration for your customer, leaving your caring nature intact.

An Example of the Sympathetic Ask

Lacy, I hear your concern about how much time this will take and how much it costs, and I know you want results now. While it does take time, it's been my experience (and my customers' experience) that when people try to take a shortcut they spend more time, energy, and money in the end, because they have to backtrack. After customers complete my program, they all tell me they would pay ten times the price I charge because of the results they get.

I know this feels like a stretch for you, but I also know going through the process, as it's designed produces the results you're looking for. If you think this is right for you, then the sooner we get started the sooner you'll get what you want. What do you say?

Primary Archetype

The Sympathetic Ask was designed for the Humanitarian Archetype. She gets to show she cares by overcoming the customer's immediate concern. The Humanitarian feels good about herself because she is helping while she asks for the business. The Sympathetic Ask allows the Humanitarian to feel confident about the value her customers get in an easy and casual style.

The Sympathetic Ask Formula

(Name), I hear your concern about _____ and know you want _____. Even though it does _____, based on my other customers' results, you are going to reduce _____ (repeat the concern) and increase _____ (repeat what they want) right away. Does that help you understand better how this works? The sooner we get started the sooner you get what you want. What do you say?

☐ The Irresistible Ask

The Irresistible Ask is a much different way of asking for the business. It requires a high level of confidence. It's designed to tempt the customer into making a decision on the spot. It usually includes telling the customer what they will be missing if they don't buy. It also includes something highly desirable to make the customer's decision easier.

An Example of the Sympathetic Ask

Julie, when we first started talking, you told me you wanted to make $1,000,000. And you wanted it badly. You can look at purchasing this program two ways. First, it's an investment in getting that million bucks into your bank account, because you'll get the tools and support you need to accomplish that goal. If you don't, you'll have to figure it out for yourself, and if you knew how to do that, you already would have made $1,000,000. And second, getting this opportunity at this price is a great deal and you know it. So knowing I can help you make that money, doesn't it make sense for you to buy this program because it's really a small investment compared to your goal?

Primary Archetype

I'll bet you already determined this powerful ask is the one the Temptress Archetype could use. It's a bold and courageous style of asking and requires a seductive nature to use it successfully. It's tempting because it weaves the customer's goal throughout it and gets inside the customer's head. Because it's true, the customer cannot figure out how to disagree, which is why it works.

The Irresistible Ask Formula:

(Name), when we first started talking, you said you wanted _____ and you told me you wanted it badly. You can look at it two ways, if you decide to purchase this _____, you'll get _____ to get _____ and you know it. If you don't, you could miss out on _____, which I know isn't what you want. So knowing you want _____, doesn't _____ make sense for you?

☐ The Charming Ask

The Charming Ask is casual, fun and lighthearted. It exudes warmth and caring for the customer. The archetypes that use this ask tend to be more of a friend with their customers and less of a leader in the relationship. The Charming Ask feels like something that happens between people who know each other well, and is less forward. It can also include a little something to sweeten the pot because the asker believes an additional enticement makes everything easier. It's the type of ask that you can use until you muster up the courage for a more audacious ask.

An Example of the Charming Ask

Joy, can I tell you how much fun I had getting to know you? We seem to have connected so easily and had tons of fun. I just love how amazing you are and what you do! Now that you know more about how I customize my necklaces, can't you see how fun it would be to create this signature piece together? Just because I really like you, I will give you 15% off. Does that help make your decision?

   Note: I would recommend that you don't offer the discount unless the customer asks for it. If they do, consider staying firm on price and giving them something else they want.

Primary Archetype

The Charming Ask is used religiously by the Romantic Archetype. She loves to feels like she and her customers are friends. While the Romantic hates asking for the business, the Charming Ask allows her to preserve the carefully developed relationship with her customer while getting paid to join forces.

The Charming Ask Formula

   (Name), we have had so much fun together and you are my favorite type of customer. I just love _____ about you. Now that you've heard what _____ can do for you and we seem to bond easily, can't you see how great it would be to join forces? Because I like you so much, I will throw in a little bonus. You can have _____ if you decide to work with me. How does that sound?

☐ The Shrewd Ask

The Shrewd Ask is clever because it puts the decision-making responsibility back on the customer and allows the asker to maintain their freedom in the closing phase of the sales. This ask is commonly used when the asker feels strongly about not tampering with destiny. She wants the customer to be sure and asks them to do a "gut check" before making a final decision. If needed, it can be tailored to be more assertive and can be customized for almost any situation. The user of this ask needs to know their customer's desires well and use that information to perfect this style.

An Example of the Shrewd Ask

You know, Christina, I have told you as much as I can about this offer. You either know that you want it or you don't. Knowing that you want to create a new business for yourself, what do you see is possible based on some of the ways I could help you do that? Tell me what you see as being valuable to you in working together?

Primary Archetype

The archetype that primarily uses this ask is the Maverick. The Maverick likes her freedom so much that she wants to ensure that her customers are ready to embark on a journey together. If the customer isn't sure, the Maverick would rather maintain her ability to move on. The Shrewd Ask is also a great way to handle Ruminating Buyers, because they talk themselves into making the purchase. Now isn't that shrewd?

The Shrewd Ask Formula

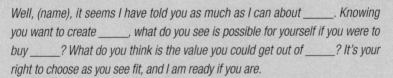

Well, (name), it seems I have told you as much as I can about _____. Knowing you want to create _____, what do you see is possible for yourself if you were to buy _____? What do you think is the value you could get out of _____? It's your right to choose as you see fit, and I am ready if you are.

5

☐ The Invitational Ask

The Invitational Ask is a subtle but powerful way to ask your customer for the business. It's like asking someone to dinner. It's a more casual way to act and is the most popular of all of the asks. It works well because it's a simple way of getting your customer to see the immense value available to them.

An Example of the Invitational Ask

Lisa, it seems like we're on to something here. Based on our conversation, it sounds like you understand that you could get exactly what you want from this product. I invite you to consider what we've discussed and decide if you're ready to buy. I'm confident you'll get amazing value for your investment, so let me know what you think.

Primary Archetype

The primary archetype that uses this close is the Nurturer. Doesn't this ask sound like something your mother or a trusted friend would say to you? The Nurturer tells you why it's good for you, doesn't push, and invites you to take the next step toward making the purchase. The Nurturer needs a gentle, warm, and effective way to ask for the business and this is it. Anyone can use this asking style.

The Invitational Ask Formula

(Name), it sounds like you're excited about using/acquiring _____. Based on what you told me, you can easily see how you would be able to _____. I invite you to _____ and check in with yourself to see if you're ready to _____. I would love to know what you think.

☐ The Encouraging Ask

The Encouraging Ask is inspirational in tone and motivates customers to take action. It's most powerful when the asker can see how different the customer's future will be after she makes the purchase. It needs to be filled with enthusiasm, compassion, and support. The Encouraging Ask doesn't work when the asker doesn't fully believe in what's possible for the customer, because it has to be heartfelt to be perceived as authentic. This is another ask anyone can use if it's customized for the situation.

An Example of the Encouraging Ask

Angela, just think, thirty days from now you could be seeing the results from this eye cream and you'll have minimized the lines around your eyes. But you have to be willing to take a leap of faith and try it. I encourage you to think about how much you want to look younger before you make your final decision. It works for me, and it can work for you, too. What do you think?

Primary Archetype

It's no doubt, this asking style fits the Visionary Archetype most naturally. See how she is able to tell how the future result will alleviate the customer's current desire? She tells the story of how the product's benefit gives the customer exactly what she wants and more. She captures the customer's heart by appealing to the part of her that wants to look younger. She is also talking to her brain, suggesting it needs to make a choice or the heart won't get what it wants.

The Encouraging Ask Formula

(Name), just think, _____ from now you could be experiencing _____. But you have to be willing to take a leap of faith. I encourage you to consider _____ before you make your final decision. Any thoughts about what I just said?

☐ The Perceptive Ask

The Perceptive Ask requires a conscious connection to the customer and her dilemma. It requires the asker to go beyond what she hears the customer saying and tune into her inner guiding voice. The Perceptive Ask comes from a deep place inside, from the soul. When using the Perceptive Ask, see if you instinctually feel as though a new truth or awareness has emerged about what the customer needs to hear that will aid her decision. The Perceptive Ask is very powerful for those who are naturally intuitive about other's needs.

An Example of the Perceptive Ask

Brenda, I am getting the sense there's something more than just money you want to experience from your business. Is that accurate? (She replies.) Well, knowing that you want more work-life balance as well as more income, I recommend you consider this package, because it's designed specifically to help you create a plan for making all the money you want while maintaining a healthy work style. Given that this package satisfies your needs, doesn't this sound like the best fit for you?

Primary Archetype

The Mentor Archetype uses the Perceptive Ask most often. She is completely in tune with her customers' deepest desires and has vision into the heart of the matter. She is able to speak the truth to her customers because she comes with a world of experience and credibility. Because she wants her customer to get the highest and best value out of doing business together, she calls it as she sees it. To perfect her natural ask, the Mentor likes to make a recommendation and clarify which choice would be the best for the customer.

Note: Customers appreciate specific recommendations, so feel free to add this part to your natural ask.

The Perceptive Ask Formula

(Name), I'm getting the sense that _____ and based on what I am hearing you say is _____. Is that accurate? (Let them answer.) What I want to let you know is _____ and you can have exactly what you want. I recommend _____ because _____. Doesn't this sound like the ideal solution for you?

☐ The Heartfelt Ask

The Heartfelt Ask is sincere, gentle, and clear. It's empathetic in nature because it includes the asker's own inspirational story. It works well because it speaks to the customer's heart and opens them to new possibilities. It instantly has a positive effect because it takes the customer out of her head and into her emotions. The person who uses the Heartfelt Ask is passionate about saving her customers. It's similar to holding out a helping hand, and customers respond well to that type of care. The key to using this asking style is to speak your genuine truth and explain the positive outcome.

An Example of the Heartfelt Ask

Jamie, I can feel how much you've struggled with regaining your sensuality after such a traumatic experience. I created this product because my heart was aching from watching so many suffer from the same problem. I know deep in my heart this is what you've been looking for and it will make you feel feminine again. It worked for me. Won't you try it?

Primary Archetype

The Heartfelt Ask is the Heroine's favorite way of winning the business. She wants so badly to help her customers, she appeals to them by speaking the truth of what is in her heart. It hits home with customers because they feel supported enough to trust her and make a decision. This is one of the best asks anyone can use. It's powerful, and its power grows the more genuine you are. The asker must feel a deep level of compassion and empathy for your customer's situation or it comes off as insincere.

The Heartfelt Ask Formula

(Name), I can feel how much you (have struggled/want) _____. I developed _____ because my heart _____. I know with every fiber of my being _____ and you can feel _____. It worked for me. Won't you try it?

9

☐ The Enlightened Ask

The Enlightened Ask is about two missions coming together helping to fulfill the other. The asker that uses the Enlightened Ask appeals to the customer's higher purpose, asking them to join forces based on a cause greater than profit. Yes, it caters to the buyer's sensibilities, but it also encourages the customer to buy for spiritual reasons. The asker that uses this approach only wants to do business with people who support her cause or movement.

An Example of the Enlightened Ask

Susan, by carrying this line of eco-friendly clothing, you'll be giving your customers what they want, which in turn makes you money. Even more important than that is you and I will be one step closer to helping people become more conscious about taking care of the planet. Not to mention, the money you spend with me supports global artists who need a break. It seems our higher aspirations complement each other. Does it feel in alignment to place an order? (Or: Are you ready to place and order and do some good together?)

Primary Archetype

You've probably guessed that this ask is most often used by the Mystic Archetype. She loves to remind everyone about the bigger payoff of having dual, compatible missions. She loves nothing more than to be able to inspire a transaction that has more meaning than money. The Mystic wants to know each dollar that exchanges hands is doing good for someone or something else. That is what inspires her to be in business.

The Enlightened Ask Formula

(Name), by deciding to buy _____, you'll be serving your customers more fully, which in turn (list the customers benefit) _____. Even more important, by joining forces we _____. It seems as though our _____ are complementary. Why don't we _____ together.

☐ The Delicate Ask

The Delicate Ask is a much softer asking style than some of the others. It's for sensitive types who don't ever think asking for business is appropriate for them. The Delicate Ask can be used creatively and have plenty of impact. It's a gentle approach for those who want to handle their customers carefully and keep themselves as far away from the selling process as possible. It works well for people who loathe asking for money, thinking it diminishes their spirit or brand.

An Example of the Delicate Ask

Lynn, you know I'm not one to push, and I operate from my creative self most of the time. I design for people like you who also want to be expressive. What I've noticed is that those who have learned from me before have seen an increase in their business because they're more joyful. This is always awkward for me to do, but I have to ask you, would you be interested in taking this program/workshop?

Primary Archetype

Sounds exactly like an Artist, doesn't it? Because Artists are highly creative, they can be sensitive, which is often perceived by customers as being easily offended. Artists want to ensure that their customers know they are aware of their feelings. Artists don't want anything to do with the sales process. The way for them to keep asking for the business is to tell the truth about how asking makes them feel. The Delicate Ask allows the artist to be creative with words and remain free from being perceived as a "gross salesperson." Anyone can use this ask, just know that it's the softest approach; you may have to work a little harder to get the result you want.

The Delicate Ask Formula

(Name), you know I'm not one to push and I operate from my creative side most of the time. I designed/made/created _____ for _____ who want _____. Of the people who have bought/participate in they tend to _____. Would you be interested in _____?

☐ The Illumined Ask

The Illumined Ask is straightforward and addresses the customer's issue upfront. The asker, in this case, has already decided this customer needs her products and services so much, she won't take no for an answer. While it may seem too aggressive, this ask leads the customer to see exactly how they will benefit from working with the asker. The Illumined Ask builds trust, loyalty, and respect in the relationship because it's direct and frank.

An Example of the Illumined Ask

Joy, you came to me because you can't figure out to set up your business to reflect how great your work is. The problem I see is that you aren't clear about what you really want to do. If you were clear, you would know exactly how to construct your programs and you would save time fumbling around. I know you are frustrated, and when we work together you'll get the vision you crave and a business you love. I see so much potential for you, but we cannot get started until you let me know if you are ready.

Primary Archetype

The archetype that heads straight for the heart of the problem and envisions a positive outcome for the customer is the Liberator Archetype. This ask plays to her natural ability to see the potential in her customer that the customer does not yet see in herself. She affirms what is possible by telling the customer exactly what needs to change and how it will manifest the desired result. It's more direct than some of the other asks. The Illumined Ask is very effective, and if you can learn to use it properly, winning business will be easier.

The Illumined Ask Formula

(Name), you came to me because _____ and you want _____. The main thing I see you struggling with is _____. If you could improve/overcome _____ you would be able to _____. I know you feel _____ and when you are ready to make that change, together we can _____. Can we agree this is the right course of action for you?

☐ The Proof Ask

The Proof Ask is exactly what it sounds like: a logical approach that speaks to the customer's brain. It tells the customer precisely how they will accomplish their goals by using an information, data, or math example. It's commonly used to demonstrate how a customer will make their money back, thus justifying the investment. The Proof Ask is also useful on a webpage or shopping cart, when you cannot speak to your customer. It uses tools such as testimonials and client success stories. The Proof Ask can also be combined with another ask or used as a backup when you have a reluctant customer.

An Example of the Proof Ask

Sally, humor me for a minute and let's walk through this example. I think you'll see just how easy earning back your investment will be. Let's say you buy this book-writing mentorship program and spend $3,500 with me. First, you are going to feel elated because you'll have finished writing your book. Second, if you make $10 a copy, you only need to sell 350 copies to break even. You and I both know it's much more likely you'll sell a couple thousand copies. If we take 2,000 copies times $10 a book, that totals $20,000 in your bank account! If we deduct the cost of this course, you net $16,500 profit! Don't you think that sounds like an investment worth making? If you don't finish the book, you won't make anything. Can you see how the upfront expense is worth it?

Primary Archetype

It's pretty clear the Sassy Savant will love using this type of ask. The Proof Ask allows her to showcase her intelligence. She also gets to win over her customer, build trust, and gain loyalty. The customer loves the Proof Ask because she can see clearly how making this investment will positively impact her future. If you're selling a product or service that will directly affect someone's income, this is the perfect ask to use. The Sassy Savant will make the Proof Ask her own by adding in a tiny bit of wit.

The Proof Ask Formula

(Name), let me explain how you can make back your money. Let's say you buy _____ for the cost of _____. If you get to keep _____ per _____, then you need to sell _____ (divide the cost per unit into the cost of what you are selling) to break even. Knowing that you want to make more than that, you need to sell _____ of units to make _____. Doesn't that sound like a no-brainer way to get what you want? Not to mention feeling _____!

Isn't it fun to see how many different ways there are to ask for the business? And did you notice how each one was conversational? Selling is simply a conversation between two people interested in working together. It's natural for a discussion to occur or the customer has no way of evaluating your offer. Experiment with them. As you become more comfortable asking for the business, you'll likely use pieces from different asks, creating your own custom asking style.

These natural asking styles also help you handle objections! Let's take a closer look at how to do that.

Overcoming Objections

I am sure you've heard the term "overcoming objections." It sounds so formal and yet the need to do it occurs all the time. Earlier in this book, we talked about the decision-making process. Objections arise as your customers switch between their head and their heart, trying to decide what to do. It's normal. In truth, customers aren't really objecting, or saying no, as much as they're trying to prove to themselves buying is a good decision. They are, in fact, asking you to help them justify spending the money.

Here is one of my absolute favorite secrets to reveal. It shocks most people when they first hear it, but after it sinks in they agree it's true. Ready? Customers only object when they're considering buying from you. They don't object if they're already sure it's not for them.

> **Customers only object when they're considering buying from you.**

Why would a customer waste one minute of anyone's time, including their own, if they were not interested in buying your product or service? Only interested customers who are mulling over a decision object!

Now that you know customers only object when they're interested, you should feel immediate relief and a surge in confidence because knowing this makes it easier to overcome an objection. Objections aren't something to be afraid of; they're something to embrace. They're a strong indicator that the customer wants to buy what you are selling.

If we start thinking of an objection as a buy signal, the most important piece is not the objection itself, it's the unresolved issue behind the objection. Your job is to ask questions until you know exactly why the customer is unable to choose. Here are some possibilities:

- Sometimes customers' resistance patterns emerge if what you are selling means they have to change.
- Sometimes customers hesitate because they don't understand how they're going to get value equal or greater to the cost.
- Sometimes customers have to discuss it with someone else, like a spouse, and aren't clear how to justify the purchase.
- And sometimes, customers are just slow decision-makers.

The idea is to uncover what is holding the customer up from making a decision. Your ability to help them resolve their decision-making challenge is how you get to be of service to them. It's the first stage of helping them get what they want. Buying your product or service is the second stage of helping them enhance their life.

When you know what is beneath the hesitancy, you can explain what is unclear or provide more information. If you don't know what is stopping them, you'll waste time and energy in an attempt to overcome an obscure conflict.

Think of it this way: Imagine you are talking to a friend and you noticed something was bothering them. You would ask what has upset or confused them, right? And your friend would appreciate your concern and tell you.

It's the same thing with a customer. They will be grateful you are taking the leadership role and that you care enough to ask what is stopping them. It shows you are interested in them as a person more than making the sale. And it's the difference between being "salesy" versus being of service.

I personally love objections because it points out the holes in my sales story. When I find one of those holes, I plug it the next time around to avoid having to handle the same objection. It became another of my secret weapons. My customers respected my ability to anticipate their concerns long before they expressed them. Because this technique further establishes a trusted bond with customers, the effortless yes becomes a frequent event.

Ways to Handle Objections

As I have said, objections occur in a variety of ways. You never know what mental or emotional hurdles will surface for your customer. You have to be able to tap dance a little bit and use the skill of intuitive listening to reveal the hidden conflict. Do everything you can to dig up the issue that is stopping the sale, and you will have unlocked the secret to making more than you'll ever need.

Here are a few simple steps you can take to overcome and handle objections that arise. Use these steps after you have asked for the business the first time.

If the customer is hesitant, ask what they're thinking or what is causing them to be uncertain. Let them answer. You might say, "I notice you don't seem as excited as you did earlier. Is there something stopping you from making a final decision?" Or, "Something has shifted around your energy, is something not making sense?"

Once you know what the issue is you can address it. Review the twelve natural asking styles and determine which one would work best in this specific situation. You can also stick with your most natural style and rephrase it based on this new information.

If you are able to resolve their issue, you should be able to win the business. If it works but another concern comes up, use a natural ask again, this time phrasing it so it addresses the current conflict. Keep repeating as this step as many times as needed.

If you have made an honorable attempt to handle any or all objections multiple times and the customer is stuck on one point and won't let it go, try using the "other perspective ask" where you reach a natural point in the conversation and can agree to disagree. This strategy can help them to be more open-minded and consider another point of view. (It works with spouses, too!)

You might say something like, "Betty, I hear that you don't believe

_____ is possible. I have to disagree with you. What I have seen happen with my customers who use _____ to its fullest potential is _____ or they produce _____ results. There isn't much more I can say. I guess we have to agree to disagree."

Be quiet and see what the customer has to say. If this doesn't work, move on to the next step.

If you've tried to handle any or all objections multiple times and are getting frustrated and would rather end this conversation, you can make one last effort to win the business and use the "walk away ask." The beauty of this ask is you get to bow out of the relationship gracefully if they don't buy. Most of the time, though, this ask gets someone off the fence and on to the playing field. Ninety percent of the time it unlocks a stalemate.

You might say something like this. "Betty, I think we are starting to get frustrated with each other. I have done the best I can to explain the value and benefits to you. Maybe this isn't the right time or the right fit for you. It's not a problem and I hope we can leave on good terms." Be quiet and let the customer talk. If they really truly want what you are selling, they will run back and let you know it. If they agree with you then they weren't meant to be your customer and now you are both free!

Once you know what is causing your customer to hesitate, you can follow the steps outlined above and use any of the twelve natural asks to aid the customer's decision-making process. My hope for you is that by being exposed to and becoming aware of the many styles you could use to ask for the business as well as the steps you can take to overcome objections, you will never be stumped again. Using these techniques is how you get to become a falter-free seller. How great would that be for your self-esteem and bank account?

If the customer is worried about the cost or doesn't have the money, the next section will tell you in more detail how to handle that specifically.

It's Never About the Money

The most common objection heard around the world is, "I cannot afford it," "It's out of my budget," or "It's too expensive." Are you ready for another secret? When a customer objects to price, it's never about the money. Ever. Period.

People use the money objection because they don't know what else to say and it's the easiest way to get you to retreat. The money objection erects a protective barrier around the customer so they can hide from making a decision.

When you buy into a customer's money story, they have effectively sold you on why they cannot buy what you are selling and have flipped the script on you. Avoid getting caught up in their money conversation because it's a black hole, costing you precious dollars.

Instead, realize there is something beneath their objection to the price and find out what that is. If you are a coach, your first assignment is to coach them past their objection. It's a great way for your customer to experience your work style. Use your coaching skills to help remove this barrier for your customer.

If you are selling a product, you know everything there is to know about it. Ask your customer why they perceive the price to be something they cannot fathom. Then you will find out the real reason they're hesitating. Use your knowledge to help dispel their belief.

There are some translations you should be aware of so dealing with the money objection isn't so daunting. First, when someone says, "I cannot afford it," it can mean any number of things.

It can mean, "I don't really want to change so that is my excuse for ending this conversation." Or it can mean "Are you crazy? I don't have the money in my bank account to do that."

This is where it gets a tiny bit tricky. You have to determine if they're objecting because your offer is really outside of their price range or if they're reluctant because it would require them to change and they're resisting. Sometimes the ego will kick in and create a limiting financial scenario to slow things down.

Start asking questions. Get them to tell you why they think they cannot afford it. The key is to find out if they want the program and cannot justify the expense, if their resistance to change has reared its head, or if they don't want the program and are using money as the excuse instead of just telling you it's not a fit. The conversation might go something like this:

Cannot-Afford-It Example

You: Tell me why you think you cannot afford it.

Customer: I just don't have it in the bank and I have never spent that much before on something like this.

You: Let's pretend you had the money, would you want to buy this?

Customer: Yes, I just don't see how to come up with the cash.

You: So to be clear, money is the only thing stopping you from signing up, is that what you are saying?

Customer: Yes. I don't have it.

You: What if we were to brainstorm for a minute and talk about what you could do to get the money. Any ideas occur to you?

Customer: Well, I could make payments. I could ask to borrow the money. I do have some savings for my business. Or I could sell _____ and make it.

You: Those are some great ideas. Does one of them strike you as the solution or get you excited?

Customer: I like the idea of selling _____. I need to do that anyway. Tell you what, I will run a promotion with the intention of raising enough money to pay for this program and get back to you.

You: That sounds like a great idea. You know that investing in this program and committing to do it now is the same as setting a strong intention. If you were to put down a deposit, it would let the higher powers know you are serious. It would also keep you accountable. If you wanted to do that, I would be more than happy to help you spread the word about your promotion.

(*Note:* you can always use one of the twelve natural asking styles once you know what is really behind their money objection.)

The Resistance Example

You: Tell me why you think you cannot afford it.

Customer: I just don't have the money.

You: Let's pretend you had the money, would you want to buy this?

Customer: Yes and no. I like what I am hearing, but it seems like the process is too time consuming for me right now.

You: Okay, so it sounds to me like the money isn't really the issue. It's that you don't have the time to commit to this right now?

Customer: Yes, that is more of the issue. I am too busy right now and want to get the most out of this program.

You: If I could ask, are you always this busy or is this a temporary situation.

Customer: Well, I am always this busy, now that you ask. That seems to be the norm with me.

You: Based on what you are telling me, it sounds like being too busy is exactly the problem you want to resolve. And, if this is normal for you, there isn't ever going to be a slower time, so why not now?

Customer: You raise a really good point. I think that is my excuse for staying stuck or in limbo. Now that you have me thinking about it, is that something we could work on?

You: Yes, and I think this issue is what is in your way in all areas of your life. It's the way you have been making choices that don't serve you. How would you feel about getting started two weeks from now? That would give you some time to get things off your plate and plan for our time together.

Customer: You know, I like that idea. Could I make payments since I need to pay off some other things?

Do you see how this was not about money once we were able to dig a little deeper? This was about her resistance coming up and relying on her "I'm too busy" excuse. Usually when the customer says something like that, it's the very excuse that creates the situation they want to resolve. Find a delicate and warm way to get them to see that.

Customers might also give you the "It's Too Expensive" objection.

What is interesting about this objection is they aren't saying they don't have the money to buy it, they're saying they don't see how the cost will translate into value that exceeds the price. Can you see how this particular objection isn't about money already? It's about value. It's about how they will see the return on the investment related to their unique circumstances. You have to revisit and restate your unique payoff proposition. If that doesn't work, it's time to probe a bit deeper. That conversation might sound something like this:

The It's-Too-Expensive Example

You: That is interesting you say that. Tell me why you think it sounds too expensive.

Customer: Well, to be honest, I don't see how I can justify the cost.

You: So tell me, is it that you haven't ever spent this kind of money before and that is making you nervous, or is it that you don't see how you can make your money back?

Customer: Great question.

See how this could go either way?

If they answer they have never spent this much money before, restate your unique payoff proposition as one of the twelve natural asks, and this time be specific.

If they say they cannot see how the value is worth the price, use the Proof Ask to demonstrate how they make their money back. You could also tell them a true story about one of your customer's successes with your product or service. Remember to keep that customer's name confidential.

By now I am sure you can see clearly why it's never about the money. Using money as an excuse is a great way for the customer to create a dead-end street. If you don't probe and find out what the real story is, you end up leaving money on the table. It also becomes a negative experience for your customer because they cannot find a way out of their dilemma.

The twelve natural asking styles provide you with a vast array of tools to naturally handle any obstacles that occur during the sales process. They're easy to use. Just dust off your moxie. They also help your archetype develop stronger muscles. If you find yourself having to lead a team, they should read this book, too. Not only will these seven steps to the Effortless Yes make you all the money you'll ever need, they also make you a more effective business owner, relationship builder, and manager.

With that said, it's time to put all the steps together and become bankable for life.

Exercises

1. Pick the natural ask you would like to start using. Using its formula, write it two or three different ways.
2. Pick your second favorite asking style and write out at least one example using that formula. The more examples you write out, the easier it will be to use them on the spot. Before you know it, you will be asking without having to stress about it.
3. Pick the most common money story you get and write out two to three different ways you would handle it. If you do this exercise now instead of waiting until the next time you hear it, you will be falter-free when speaking directly with your customer.
4. Practice by role-playing with your friends, staff, or anyone else who can give you constructive feed back.
5. Make a commitment to regularly ask for the business, and watch your bank account grow!

10

becoming bankable

NOW THAT YOU HAVE COMPLETED the seven steps to securing the Effort-less Yes, it's time to put it all together and become bankable. For life. Becoming bankable means you possess the ability to harness the power of your brilliant and exceptional talents and turn them into purposeful, lavish, and consistent prosperity. Said another way, if a picture is worth a thousand words, then your ability to envision your bankability is worth millions and beyond. Being bankable means no more winging it. Is it possible? I'm here to tell you it is!

When you start using some of the smart tools that the big boys of business use, you will find all the money you'll ever need. It's already inherent in your business, waiting for you to be ready to receive it. When you do, you can retain your earnings and build up your net worth immediately. Sellebrate! You can win business more frequently. Yeah! You can stop putting every dollar you make back into ex-penses. Phew! You can make more than your life costs. WooHoo! You can live the life you always dreamed of. Finally! Isn't this why you went into business for yourself? To feel joyful, elated, and free? This is what becoming bankable is all about.

I did it and so can you ... but you have to do the work and put the tools into use every day.

First, you make a plan, because that is where you will find the excess dollars in your business and put them in the bank. Next, follow the seven steps of the Effortless Yes! Selling System and win more and more business, graciously and effortlessly. You also have to set your prices so they're fair *and* profitable. And finally, you have to choose to have the mindset, heart set, and skill set of a bankable entrepreneur.

There is only one person who can stop running your business impulsively, and that is you. You will need to look at your numbers. The big boys of business are consistently bankable because they focus intently on growth. They look at their numbers, as painful or as joyful as that may be. They're unwilling to compromise their financial security, and they don't let discomfort about numbers stop them. Nor should it stop you.

You will have to look at your numbers if you want to become bankable. But you are different than those big boys of business who want to profit more than they want to fulfill a bigger purpose. Your business has your heartfelt passion built into the core of your offering. Becoming bankable is all about balancing your mission with your ultimate payoff, so it feels good to you *and* your customers. If you don't pay attention to your cash flow, how can you get where you want to go? Or know if your business has grown?

Your financial statements are like a garden. Your money needs care, watering, weeding, fertilizing, and pruning. Most people avoid looking at their sales numbers and income because they don't want to get upset or see how little they have made. They also avoid looking at how much they've spent because the net result is not what they want to see.

But business *is* defined by the money, and if you avoid looking at your sales numbers and income you will not prosper. Money is the life force of a business, and without it you can't do the greater good you set out to do. Not only are you missing where you could be saving money (pruning) but you are also missing the hidden opportunities that represent the big payoffs (fertilizing). Instead, most of you are addicted to bypassing the most important information you have about your state of freedom, the tangible numbers.

> **Money is the life force of a business, and without it you can't do the greater good you set out to do.**

I know it's intimidating to review the money that flows in and out of your business. It can seem extremely daunting and make you feel ill. I get it. I also suggest to you that you aren't owning the greatness of your talents nor are you clearly seeing how much you earn if you don't look. Achieving purposeful prosperity is an intention. To make an intention real, you have to stay committed to it and be willing to assess your progress toward realizing it.

Becoming bankable is about making more than you'll ever need. To do that you have to understand what your business costs you and build from there. The big picture of what is possible is your large goal. How you accomplish that large goal is to plan how to get there by dividing the goal into chunks. You must never forget where the chunks are taking you; it's why you focus your attention on the large goal instead of one chunk at a time.

For example, if I want to make $500,000 and keep $350,000 of that, it means my expenses are $150,000. At the end of the year, I want my sales numbers to be $500,000 or above. I plan to get to the $500,000 by selling various chunks of whatever I offer. My big goal is $500,000, and the total of the chunks equals or exceeds that large goal. Too many entrepreneurs make the mistake of only focusing on the amounts they need to get by and never planning where they ultimately want to go.

The chunks represent part of how you get to the large goal. They're often mistaken as the goal itself, which is why so many people break even or lose money every year. That type of thinking gets you stuck in the transactional mindset. If you want to be bankable and create a cash-rich business, you will switch your mindset to real-

The Eleven Bankable Beliefs

1. You trust there is more than enough for you and your business.
2. You claim your sweet spot, own the value and worth you provide, and vibrate with your natural brilliance.
3. Your business model includes you being financially supported to live your ideal life.
4. You are highly attuned to who is your ideal customer and who is not, and you honor that.
5. Your intention is to always provide tremendous value, knowing it's natural for you to be paid lavishly in exchange.
6. Your prices reflect a balance between what you really want to get paid and the optimum outcome your customers receive.
7. You consciously and gratefully give back in service to your divine mission.
8. You are always kind, caring, and respectful to those with whom you come in contact.
9. You are focused on and committed to making all you'll ever need.
10. You are emotionally intact as you build a sustainable, reliable, and consistently cash-rich business. And if not, you stop and take care of yourself.
11. You use the Effortless Yes! system to graciously and consistently win business.

ize the large goal is where you are going and chunks are going to take you there. That is how you create lavish income, by envisioning the totality of your bankability! Make sense?

To become bankable, three things must align. The first is your "mindset," the thought process that has you taking appropriate action toward attracting the money you want. The second is your "heart set," the infusion of your business with your higher purpose and deep caring for your customers. The third is your "skill set," the use of the Effortless Yes! seven-step selling system to winning business graciously. When your mindset, heart set, and skill set are working together on the shared ultimate purpose—helping your customers and achieving your big goal—you step into a new paradigm, that of becoming bankable. A paradigm of your own making. One that you get to design and create based on your needs and wants. A paradigm limited only by your imagination.

Thankfully with the downturn of the economy in 2007, we moved into a new era of entrepreneurship, which leveled the playing field. It's widely acceptable to create your business model exactly as you like.

To support you in bringing your mindset, heart set, and skill set into cooperative alignment, I developed eleven bankable beliefs. These beliefs harmonize your mind, your heart, and the new skills you have learned, to increase your likelihood of becoming bankable.

Now that you know the bankable beliefs, you can post them where you will see them. Review them and use them to keep the juices flowing and to stay positive as you build your empire. Becoming bankable is easier than you might think, but there are some things you can do to make it become reality sooner.

Releasing Transactional Thinking

One of the biggest challenges I see for female entrepreneurs is the constant tripping over the cash-generating functions of their businesses. The biggest small-business booby trap is thinking about cash flow from a transactional perspective. What this means is that you only think about how you will make the next amount of money that will save you and don't think beyond that. You get trapped in what I call the cash-quickie cycle. And it's a vicious one. I know because I used to do it religiously, and it cost me my adrenal system. It burns you out and exhausts the energy you might otherwise spend on your family or profitable creative ideas.

The cash-quickie cycle works like this: You feel panicked about some monetary situation, like paying an expensive bill. The panic motivates you to generate the cash you need to pay the bill. Once the bill is paid, you breathe, exhale, and calm down. Then the next financial pressure shows up and you repeat the process. Because you spend energy being panicked and pushing to make instant money, you burn out. You become so exhausted you neglect to find a way to generate consistent cash. Panic becomes your driving force to generate sales. You might even start to resent your business because you work furiously and are still stuck in the same financial place. And then you wonder why someone as smart as you feels lost, alone, and desperate. I know, I've been there, done that. It hurts, and it's not what you signed up for.

The truth is you aren't alone, but you *can* step out of this cycle. When you focus on the amount you need in the moment, you take your focus off the big picture. The real number you want to make. The large goal. The profitable one. Not only is it unhealthy, but you don't have a viable business if you chase cash every time the bills come in or you want to buy something. Making sales profitably is an ongoing journey and not an event.

Many wealth consciousness teachings say to "chunk it down" so that making the money you want feels easy to do. The confusion comes in because it's common to replace the large goal, or bigger picture, with a series of chunks. In order to manifest the big money, you have to know what that number is for you, intend to earn it, and use the smaller portions (chunks) as a way to get there. Your bigger number, or the source of your focus, has to include more than you need or you will be doing the cash-quickie scenario for the rest of your life, and its the source of immense pain.

Can you see how much transactional thinking is costing you? It diminishes your vitality as well as your ability to take care of yourself and those you love. It isn't sustainable. It certainly isn't reliable. It absolutely isn't dependable. It truly isn't bankable.

A cash-rich business, however, leaves you emotionally intact so you can build an empire that takes care of you. Isn't that the entrepreneurial dream? Let's make a plan the big boys use and build immense wealth.

A Simple and Smart Strategy

An important part of becoming bankable is setting your intention to do so. Intentions are powerful ways to bring into existence those things you desire. I have found that making a plan significantly helps bring your intention to life. When you can see it, it's easier to have it.

Envisioning your bankability is worth millions and beyond. In addition, the universe takes you much more seriously because you took a step beyond setting the intention and mapped out exactly how it can happen. You proved it to yourself. I always tell my clients that making a plan is the most poignant intention you will ever make.

That said, creating a plan feels heavy and burdensome. I am not a big fan of doing them either. When I start to feel that the commitment is too big or that I don't want to be responsible for achieving the big goal, I know my internal rebel voice is taking over and she isn't the one who should be running my business.

When I think back, I realize the reason my team and I were able to generate over $40,000,000 in one year at MSN during the Internet bubble was because we collectively made a plan and figured out how it was possible. Guess what? The big boys of business do this all the time. So should you. The planning is important because your business becomes predictable and reliable. It eases the fear and uncertainty that many entrepreneurs and solo-preneurs feel. From a spiritual and purpose-driven sense, making a plan demonstrates your sincerity to realizing your intention.

By all means make a vision board. Write affirmations. Create a wish list. And write a plan. It can be a smart and simple plan. I, too, hated making plans and reviewing performance spreadsheets. It was how I was evaluated for years. But then something shifted my perspective and I realized it was a way to watch my income grow. When you focus on your numbers from that point of view, you are envisioning your bankability. You get to watch your garden grow, and nurture and care for it as it needs tending. Remember we said when you envision your bankability, you bring it to life, make it real, and transform that image into real, purposeful prosperity? It's true.

Together, step-by-step, we are going to create your new year-long plan. Here is what I would like you to do:

- Add up all your expenses from the previous year. Don't make any assessments or judgments about what it cost you to run your business. Let it go.

- If you know about an upcoming expense that is not included in last year's costs, estimate how much that will be and add it to find your total expense. Now take that number and increase it by 25 percent. That new number, expenses from last year plus 25 percent, plus any upcoming expenses, is your expense projection for the new plan you are about to create.
- Next, write down how much money you want to keep based on your new plan. Don't edit that number. Think carefully about how much you would love to deposit in your personal bank account. What would get you excited? How much do you want to keep? Right now do not be concerned with whether you think that number is "doable." Just be honest with yourself, and write down what you truly want to keep. Remember, we are setting an intention for your business. What is that number?
- Now take your projected expenses total and add it to the amount you want to keep. That new total is your monetary intention for the next year of business.
- Congratulations, you have just taken the first step toward focusing your attention on making more than you need! Stand up and take a bow or dance to your favorite song because this is cause for sellebration!

Okay, now that we know how much revenue you need to generate in this year, we need to construct a way to get there. You can use a spreadsheet or write on paper. It doesn't matter. Make monthly columns, one for each month of the year. Knowing what you know about your sales cycle from last year, put a star next to those months that are typically the highest sales months. Now, put a dash next to those months that are the lowest sales months. Make a list of the reasons for your cyclical highs and lows. You will want to understand what causes the fluctuation in your income. If you plan correctly, you can learn to maximize the flows and minimize the ebbs.

Take your total revenue number and divide it up by month, taking into account high and low sales months. Think about promotional ideas you could use to help low sales months as well as boost high sales months higher. Anticipate the natural fluctuation in your business and be prepared to outsmart it. You can also use low sales months to take a break and do other things, but build those ideas into your plan. It's okay if you don't know exactly what you will sell each month. Be mindful we are doing more than making a financial plan, we are setting a clear intention for your cash flow. Just keep going. Use this planning process to get excited about creating a cash-rich future. Use it for your upliftment and growth.

Keep playing with the numbers, month-by-month, until you are able to reach your ultimate goal number. Voila! Now you have a beginning plan. You can take it a step further and figure out how much of each of your products or services you have to sell each month to meet or exceed your goal. If you take this step, you will get the extra credit; you will see precisely how you can make your overall goal and solidify it in your mind. By creating this plan, you will find "extra money" hidden in your business that you couldn't see because you never took the time to look. Feel free to increase your overall number and create a new plan if that feels like the right thing to do.

Doesn't it feel better to plan a cash-rich future instead of being stuck implementing the cash-quickie strategy? You are clearly setting your intention to manifest the income you truly want to make. This is how it's done. This is how you create a stronger sense of security for yourself. But you have to be willing to take the time and thought to build your plan.

One last thing about making a plan: things don't always go according to plan, but you should be used to that by now. The point is that you put your commitment and intention down on paper. You see how what you want is truly possible. That is priceless. What matters most is that you watch your business grow and acknowledge yourself and bless every customer. It's about your spiritual growth and development anyway. Stop winging it and making yourself repeat patterns that no longer serve you. That is the key to becoming bankable and doing so with heart.

Course Correcting

If you like where this is leading and are excited about the cash-rich possibilities you see come to life, do what most big businesses do and compare your sales plan to actual sales generated. Before you roll your eyes and throw this book at the wall, think about how committed you are to making the number you wrote down. Do you really want it? Do you feel energized and unstoppable? Are you willing to do what it takes to get there? Or are you unhappy and want to make a new plan? Do what you need to do to get excited about becoming bankable. Now let's take the next step, the step that will make the difference between wishing you could make that much and making that much.

Each month, look at your plan and compare what you planned to sell to what you actually sold. When you do this, you become mature in the way you run your business. You start to notice where you are in the overall scheme of creating money. Even better, you start to find new fruitful ways to nurture your business and overcome slumps.

Depending on what your comparison tells you, correct your course and stay on track. If you neglect to review your numbers, it sends a message to the universe that you don't truly care about the monetary intention you created. Taking this step and being willing to course correct when you get off track is game changing. It also opens up the creative juices as you mature and transform your company as needed.

Do you want to know a well-kept secret? When you look at your plan and watch your progress closely, you get to see what you could be doing better as well as acknowledge how much you have improved! The two go together. When you avoid reviewing your numbers, you also avoid feeling elated and grateful for your progress.

As you examine your numbers, consider these questions: Did you notice any trends? Were you above or below your monthly goal? If you were below it, what happened to make that so? Do you need to do more of something or less of something in the next month? What change could you make so you can exceed your number and make up for the dip? How could you make next month more profitable?

Were you above your planned number? What do you think contributed to increased success this month? How could you repeat that next month? How could you use the momentum from this month to increase sales in a low month? What are you going to do to celebrate this positive outcome? Do you want to change anything so that things are easier in the future? What did you learn that you could use to your advantage later? How are you feeling about your plan? Do you need to tweak it or revamp it?

Keep doing this on the last working day of each month. I promise you it will be rewarding and the best education you will get. It will also translate into easy growth the following year. You will know more about your business, including its strengths and weaknesses. You will find income you didn't know was waiting to be discovered. You will find soul-satisfaction in taking care of the cash-generating part of your business as much as you find joy in helping your customers. You will be able to see the future much more clearly and know undoubtedly what is the next natural growth phase for your company.

If you are invigorated by this process and want to take it further, establish signposts to map your progress. Signposts are used to determine the direction your plan is taking. For example, you could design a signpost that says, "In ninety days I want to have increased my sales of X product or service by 20 percent." At the ninety-day mark, check if you are on target, bypassing that target or below it. Once you know where you are, you can make changes accordingly. You can use the information you gather from your signpost to establish the next one.

I guarantee that once you start tracking your business this way, you won't be able to operate without it. Big business follows these routines daily because they know getting to the ultimate goal doesn't happen overnight. It happens month by month. It takes care, attention and course correcting to realize your large goal. It also removes the unpredictability and gives you a sense of security. The only thing you do have control of is your plan, nothing else. When things happen outside of your control, you can fall back on your plan instead of panicking. If you fall off the wagon and skip your plan for a few months, dust yourself off and start using it again. You don't want to repeat the cash-quickie cycle again, do you?

One of the biggest benefits of using the plan is it keeps you out of transactional thinking. There's no better way to avoid the exhausting quagmire of transactional thinking than using your plan. It isn't all that hard to do. It takes a short amount of time each month. If you ever want to sell your business, you will know what it's worth and how much you should get. More importantly, you will feel an unbridled enthusiasm for your business and an incredible increase in your self-esteem. And that alone will attract more business your way.

Pricing and Profitability

I'm often asked about the magic pricing formula. There isn't one. However, I do have some opinions about pricing and how it should be set with an eye toward profitability. When I say profitability, I mean two things. First, your price allows you to retain a reasonable portion of the money for yourself. Second, your price should leave you emotionally happy and not feeling any resentment toward your customers about what you are getting paid. Remember we talked earlier in this chapter about a bankable mindset being emotionally intact as you build your empire? This is where that piece can be ignored if you don't listen to your internal guidance.

The common problem with price setting, especially among entrepreneurs, is you don't set the price based on what you want and deserve to make. Instead you set your price based on how much you can get and avoid the selling process. You ask yourself what you think your customer will pay instead of evaluating what the result of your product or service is worth. While this is a popular practice, it isn't always fruitful. You got into business to make money, right? Then you have to think about your prices as a way to recoup expenses, get paid for the value you provide, and take some money home.

Becoming Bankable

I think there is a sweet zone of pricing that lies somewhere between the ultimate amount you would like to get paid and what the market will bear. Sometimes where you end up is very close if not on target to your higher price. Some will tell you price setting is a function of wealth consciousness and you should be able to charge anything you want. In my experience, that doesn't work as easily as you might want. Instead, you get what you can sell.

Selling isn't defined by whether or not your prices make it easy for a customer to purchase. As you have seen, the customer's buying decision is much more complicated than a dollar amount. Thus, setting your price so you can avoid the selling conversation doesn't help you avoid anything ... except making all you ever need!

> Setting your price so you can avoid the selling conversation doesn't help you avoid anything ... except making all you ever need!

Your belief system plays a role in how much you get paid. And the Effortless Yes! Selling System helps you buy into your own sales story, because when you believe it and buy into it, so will your customers.

Pricing is a delicate balance. You have to decide if you want to help a broad number of people or if you want to help a few. You have to put a price on the invisible things you do to help your customers, such as writing follow-up emails or doing research to resolve their challenges. If you don't factor in these things, you should. As long as your booty is in a chair or your mind is focused on your customer, that time is valuable to them. Based on the bankable belief system, you agreed to be paid lavishly in exchange for the value you provide. How about including a few more dollars in your fees to account for that precious brainpower? Or the behind-the-scenes cost of your free gifts? You can increase your income just by making that change.

The other way to look at price setting is to think about what you don't want. For example, if you had a free hour instead of coaching someone, what would you do with that hour if you could do anything you wanted? How much is that hour worth to you? My free hour is worth a lot to me. I live in Hawaii and don't have to work to pay my bills. My prices are higher than most because that free hour is worth more than most are willing to pay to be coached. But that is my prerogative since I only want to work with highly motivated clients.

The worst thing you could do is set your prices by what you think your customers will pay and then resent them for paying so little. That doesn't serve anyone. You won't be emotionally intact, thus not bankable. Who wants that? It's also likely your customers will pick up on it and not buy from you again. That is a huge waste of talent and energy. It costs part of your spirit because you aren't happy. And you leave retirement money on the table. Not good.

Your price has to feel good to you. Your customers will gauge how they feel about the price based on how confident you are. What you broadcast energetically to your clients about how you feel about your prices is picked up on and sent right back to you. Believe in the value they get and set your prices so you feel like you both got a great deal! That is the magic price-setting formula.

Here are steps to setting your prices:

1. Write down how much you want to make off each unit or hour you sell. What percent of the price do you want to take home?

2. Determine what your cost of goods is. How much does an hour of your time cost? Or how much did it cost to make one unit of your product?

3. Decide if there are any invisibles you have not accounted for in the price. Think about things you do above and beyond the call of duty. If you sell a product, do you take the time to make recommendations? Should you add in a small consultant fee? If you are a coach and write up a formal business plan for your client, does your hourly rate include the time it takes you to do that? Decide if you are giving away too much for free and add in a little to each item to cover the costs of the invisibles.

4. Write down the price you think your customers will pay. Set a range including what your competitors charge, the expensive and the less expensive ones.

5. Add up your per unit price, either hourly or by product, including the items in steps number one, two and three.

6. How does that price make you feel? Is it too low for the time and care you invest? How does it compare to the range you established in step number four? Do you want to focus on volume and quantity of sales or do you want to focus on selling less at a higher price?

7. Adjust your price based on your answers to the question in step number six. How does it feel now? What percent of the money do you get to keep? Do you like that percent? Keep adjusting your price using these steps until it feels right to you.

8. Take your attention off what you think a customer will pay. I want to suggest you don't really know how much they would pay if you haven't engaged them in a gracious sales conversation. If you still set your price based on what you think is easy to sell, adjust it upwards.

9. Notice what your new price triggers in you. Are you feeling doubt or fear? Journal about it with the intention of uncovering the belief or fear that says you shouldn't charge that much. Intend to resolve it for the last time. Reframe that negative self-talk and write a new affirmation to repeat daily. Something like: I provide so much value to my customers. My prices clearly reflect the goodness they receive and they're eager to pay it.

10. If you need to, create an escalating price scale. Start charging more than you do now and work your way up to the price you truly want to charge.

11. Setting your price is something to consider carefully. If it doesn't feel right to you, it won't feel right to your customer. Don't copy prices just to validate what you charge. Use your passion for helping people and your unique payoff proposition to buy into your own sales story. Base your price from that divinely inspired place inside you. Think about how many units you would have to sell to reach your large goal. Does that change how you feel about your price? Adjust accordingly. Decide you will get your

price from your ideal customer and you will. Especially if you use the Effortless Yes! Selling System.

Pulling It All Together

As we have taken this journey together, you have been exposed to a tremendous amount of information that can change the way you do business forever. This information can have a lasting effect on your bank account. It's the way to get the sales you want and make all you'll ever need. All the techniques, strategies, skills, and steps outlined in this book are designed so you can easily and effortlessly step into being an entrepreneur with a viable and dependable business. Not everyone can say that.

Follow the steps as they're outlined. Take the time you need to get the most value out of each one. If it takes more time than you want to identify and claim your sweet spot, then so be it. If you don't spend the energy and effort where it's needed, you run the risk of having a business that you don't love or that isn't bankable.

My motto has always been: Minimize effort and maximize reward.

There are so many tools for you to utilize, have fun putting it all to use. Each step builds on the preceding one and was developed so you could believe and own your sales story.

Be gentle with yourself and make sure you take needed breaks. Practice using the material and add in something new to your sales process each month.

Lean into your archetype, and learn more about where you might be leaving money on the table. After all, it takes as much energy to close a small sale as it does to close a big one. Why not make more for your effort? My motto has always been: Minimize effort and maximize reward. It worked for me and it can work for you.

The Effortless Yes! is possible for you and your business. You get to say yes to a business you love. One that pays you well. Your customers get to say yes to you and eagerly pay you what you deserve. It can be as easy as breathing if you use the information to your advantage.

My recommendation is this: Create a beautiful book for yourself. List your sweet spot, your unique payoff proposition, write out your quick pitch, name your soial selling archetype, and include two versions of your natural ask. Make a selling manifesto for yourself. You can also turn your selling manifesto into a beautiful certificate to proudly hang on your wall. When you hire others to work on your team, make sure to show it to them. They will better understand you and your business, which enables them to do their job better.

It took me more than thirty years to learn these lessons the hard way. It took three years to figure out how to impart the information to you in a fun and exciting way. It makes my heart sing when women can let go of the false beliefs about selling and step into their entrepreneurial power.

I hope you make millions and beyond. I am truly optimistic that you are the face of new business in America and the solution to any economic woes. Be audacious and fulfill your mission by embracing the selling process. It's the best skill you could possible have in the world.

Here is to you saying an Effortless Yes! to living the ultimate bankable life that sets you free!

About the Author

Julie Steelman's credits read like a Who's Who of big-name corporate giants with Apple, Microsoft, Toyota, CBS, Sony Studios, and Universal Pictures in her Rolodex.

She generated more than $100+ million in sales during her thirty-year sales career. Julie is known as the Entrepreneur's Selling Expert, and her heart-centered selling strategies make her the go-to guru for entrepreneurial business owners who want to master the art of selling and maximize their bankability.

While selling with sincerity may not be the norm in Corporate America, it's standard practice for this maverick. Recognizing that the selling relationship starts with understanding a buyer's pain points, Julie earned a Masters Degree in Spiritual Psychology from the University of Santa Monica in 2001.

Julie's heart-led approach to selling transformed her clients' businesses. In one instance, she unlocked a two-year stalemate between a major movie studio and a popular search engine, closing a two-year, $3.5 million deal. In another example, she turned an apology meeting with one of the world's biggest brands into a long-term multimillion dollar deal, leaving with $1 million in hand.

Now retired to her personal paradise in Hawaii, living debt-free, Julie developed the easy-to-master "Effortless YES! Selling System."™ She spends her time helping business owners overcome their aversion to selling in an honest, transformational, and interactive style. Her ability to see the possibility for lifelong prosperity in her client's businesses has made her the highly sought after expert in her field.

Julie developed her own brand of selling by combining her vast sales expertise with her deep understanding of buyer psychology, seasoned with street smarts. She returned to the business arena to teach these powerful principles to entrepreneurs interested in getting the sales they want and making all the money they'll ever need.

www.JulieSteelman.com